Reality's Dark Dream

Before her appointment to the English
Faculty of the Chicago Circle campus
of the University of Illinois, Beverly
Fields taught at Lake Forest College and
Northwestern University; and it was
the latter institution from which
Mrs. Fields received her M.A and
Ph.D. degrees.

Reality's Dark Dream
Dejection in Coleridge

BY BEVERLY FIELDS

UNIVERSITY OF ILLINOIS AT CHICAGO CIRCLE

The Kent State University Press

KENT STUDIES IN ENGLISH
General Editor, Howard P. Vincent

I. *Essays on Determinism in American Literature*
Edited by Sydney J. Krause

II. *The Computer and Literary Style*
Edited by Jacob Leed

III. *Bartleby, The Scrivener: The Melville Annual*
Edited by Howard P. Vincent

IV. *Mark Twain and the Backwoods Angel*
By William Spengemann

V. *Reality's Dark Dream: Dejection in Coleridge*
By Beverly Fields

To my husband Sidney

Foreword

I have relied in steadily astonished gratitude on Kathleen Coburn's edition of the first double volume of the Coleridge notebooks since its appearance ten years ago. My indebtedness to other Coleridge scholars can be inferred from my notes; but I should like to single out Professor Griggs for his splendid edition of the letters. The resources of Deering Library at Northwestern University and of the Newberry Library in Chicago have been especially and continuingly valuable.

For help and fortitude in reading the manuscript, for jeremiads as well as encouragement, and for conversational stimuli which can never be documented, I am grateful to many friends. Since their names would form a minor epic catalog (and surprise a few), I shall forbear.

BEVERLY FIELDS
June 1967
Evanston, Illinois

Acknowledgment

The selection from *Matthew Arnold* by Lionel Trilling is reprinted by courtesy of the author and his publishers, W. W. Norton & Company. Copyright © Lionel Trilling, 1939.

Contents

1. Psychoanalysis and the Real Language of Men

A Reader of Milton must be always on his Duty: he is surrounded with sense; it rises in every line; every word is to the purpose. There are no lazy intervals: all has been considered and demands & merits observation.—Coleridge

Reading poetry has been for some time a legitimate matter of spending seasons in the full underlife of the word, where tonality, syntax, and gesture wait like Teiresias to deliver at least a part of the unforeseen truth. But despite the prophetic shades raised by the venerable New Critics as they descended into texts, traditional criticism has resisted, for the most part,[1] the methods of Freudian exploration beneath the verbal surface. This resistance sometimes takes the form of a Keatsian fear for the life of the rainbow, as though it were really true that one kind of analysis (Freudian) is more destructive than another (textual) or that esthetic values are so frail that they cannot survive attempts to account for them.

One reason for such fear may be a half-conscious awareness of the difficulties involved in trying to grasp firmly and simultaneously what appear to be discrete and therefore incompatible kinds of meaning. It is true that the difficulties of synthesis are enormous; but it is not true that meanings—textual, metaphysical, psychoanalytical—are incompatible: the very attempt to list them risks the comedy of a critique by Polonius and denies the

1

heart of everything Coleridge has taught us about the nature of
poetic symbol.

In the following chapters I hope to make an advance toward
synthesis: to examine systematically, and with the help of the
close reading of texts in the light of Freudian psychodynamics,
the development of Coleridge's verse toward the point where it
expresses fully and explicitly the feeling that has been studied in
literary history under the name of dejection, or melancholy, or
gloom, or spleen, or acedia. I choose to call the mood dejection
because that is what Coleridge called it in what I take to be his
last significant poem.

Coleridge's dejection has of course been fair game for writers
whose interests range from the quasi-psychological assumptions
of Hugh I'Anson Faussett about Coleridge's "tainted mind"
(1926) to the assumptions that persist in the present day about
the determining effects of opium on his verse. Marshall Suther,
in *The Dark Night of Samuel Taylor Coleridge*, interprets the
dejection as a religious crisis, and in a footnote which I find it
necessary to reply to, explains his reasons for disregarding the
psychoanalytic level of interpretation:

> Perhaps the primary reason for having ignored
> it is that I am capable neither of making the analysis
> myself, nor of assessing with confidence the worth
> of attempts that have been made.[2]

This disclaimer is followed by a quite detailed assessment of a
few such attempts, along with some pretty rigid strictures about
the proper application of psychoanalytic techniques to poetry
analysis. He goes on to ask what he regards as "the important
question": should either a psychoanalytic "diagnosis" or a "religious" one be held to "*supersede*" [Suther's italics] the other?
His answer is negative:

> Just as I think it would occur to no reasonable
> theologian to suppose he could fix certain limits within

which are to be found the instrumentalities of
contact between man and God, so I should think it
would occur to no reasonable psychoanalyst to
suppose that his *therapeutically oriented* [my italics]
interpretation of the facts of a man's life exhausts
the significance of those facts.[3]

Both Coleridge and Freud would surely agree that no interpretation of the "facts" of a man's life can exhaust their significance. The act of interpretation raises these "facts" to the level of symbols where they become radiant (in Joyce's sense), like an image, for example, which can "mean" everything a writer intends and more besides. The question, therefore, whether religious analysis ought to supersede Freudian analysis, or vice versa, is, as Suther suggests, irrelevant. But it is my bias that there is a relevant question not of superseding but of preceding, and that the child knows the parent before the man knows God. The metaphor of the great chain of being, like all good metaphors, is sturdy enough to survive the translation of its terms by any interested cultural relativist.

Suther's epithet "therapeutically oriented," as he attaches it to poetry explication that proceeds on a psychoanalytic base, raises another point that ought to be clarified. Fallacious notions about the relationship between mental illness and artistic creativity, which have produced the wound-and-the-bow theory as well as a flood of folklore, are perhaps the reason for Suther's belief that psychoanalytic explication of poetry is necessarily an effort to show psychosis or even neurosis. But Freud was so far from the sentimental idea of the *poète maudit* or from considering art as pathogenic that he postulated an "intermediate world of phantasy . . . sanctioned by human consent," in a context that recalls certain well-known observations of both Coleridge and Wordsworth. It was Freud's proposition that all men—not only the artist—share in this fantasy world, and that the artist's gift is to objectify, or universalize, his particular fantasy so that its expression provides for ordinary men pleasures they are unable to derive from their own fantasies. In this proposition, to be found in his *General Introduction to Psychoanalysis* (the original series of lectures delivered in Vienna in 1915-1916 and published in English, revised, in 1935), he reiterates the conviction of Wordsworth and Coleridge that the artist is a man speaking to men.

It appears that Coleridge drew his bow, as a matter of fact, in spite of his wounds, and that he put it away only when the exercise strained his psychic energy too far. In developing this argument I make two assumptions. The first is that Coleridge was telling the truth when he said in his dejection ode that he had lost the poetry-making power, but that the weight of feeling in the poem and the unusual history of its composition suggest that the power has not been defined—by Coleridge or by anybody else. The second assumption is that the considerable material not only in the verse but also in the letters and notebooks can illuminate a definition. Behind both assumptions is a conviction that the descriptive techniques of Freudian psychodynamics belong naturally in the realm of literary criticism, which traditionally studies the dynamics of mind.

Apparently the poetry-making power in Coleridge was the ability to transform his unconscious tensions into objective expression, to move freely between the conscious and unconscious parts of his experience, so that he could speak, as a man of intense sensibility, to other men, about the inescapable facts of the human situation. What he mourns in the poem about dejection is ostensibly the ability to sustain the effort of confronting, however indirectly, his unconscious experience, the dark dream that in his poetry-making he sensed was his reality. But underlying the ostensible object of mourning is a principle of virility, and this he mourned more or less steadily throughout all the verse that expresses his dejection.

The dejection itself, from which he was never wholly free, appears to be the result of the conversion of his unconscious ego-strivings, with their attendant feelings of fear and guilt, into a conscious mood that not only has a long history of social approval but that also disguises these strivings completely and successfully through its entirely opposite character. The strongest possible denial of the unconscious masculine wish to usurp power and authority is to become as a little child upon a lonesome wild. The conversion is unavoidable, partly because the energy necessary to repress prohibited emotions is so great that it drains the personality, producing the kind of fatigue which is one expressed characteristic of what Coleridge called his dejection, and partly because the conversion satisfies the passive female ego-strivings that are in tension with the fantasies of usurpation.

It seems possible to show that the reiteration and development of characteristic themes and images provide considerable unity for Coleridge's verse, early and late, although I do not propose to consider any verse later than the dejection ode; and the method of inquiry here pursued will, I think, demonstrate that the verse drama *Osorio* is more fully related to the rest of Coleridge's works than it has up to now appeared to be.

The powerful and beautiful ode called *Dejection* expresses brilliantly what is surely, although in varying degrees of intensity, a universal mood. The relationship of the mood to the loss of the poetry-making power, however, can be fully understood only by going back to its history of composition, and from there to the realization that the public poem is a massive effort to come to terms with the private pains of sleep.

2. *A Letter to——* and Other Letters

There is one thing wholly out of my Power. I cannot look forward even with the faintest pleasure of Hope, to the Death of any human Being, tho' it were, as it seems to be, the only condition of the greatest imaginable Happiness to me, and the emancipation of all my noblest faculties that must remain fettered during that Being's Life.—I dare not, for I can not: I cannot, for I dare not. The very effort to look onward to it with a stedfast wish would be a suicide, far beyond what the dagger or pistol could realize— absolutely suicide, coelicide, not mere viticide.
—Coleridge

i

On Sunday evening, April 4, 1802, at the close of a week-long visit of William and Dorothy Wordsworth at Greta Hall,[1] Coleridge composed and addressed to Sara Hutchinson a mass of verse with the title *A Letter to——*, which became the first draft of *Dejection: An Ode*. More than twice as long as the received version, this verse letter appears to be, among other things, an expression of dissatisfaction in his marriage and of love for the woman to whom it is addressed:

But thou, dear Sara! (dear indeed thou art,
My Comforter! A Heart within my Heart!)[2]

And yet it is a strange sort of love letter. Following immediately after this loving salute are two lines which thin its intensity

6

of when he wrote the poem, and turning back to the "William" of those he loved, he sent a lengthy extract to Sotheby, describing the verses as having been "written during that dejection to Wordsworth."[8] A transcript of the poem for Sir George Beaumont, assumed[9] to belong to this period between composition and publication, uses the term of address *William* instead of *Sara*. But on July 29 Coleridge wrote to Southey, quoting from the poem without any indication that it had been written "to" anyone.

Subsequent versions of the poem only make it more difficult to determine who the ultimate object of this expression of intimate feelings was. For its first publication, in the *Morning Post* on October 4, Coleridge trimmed the poem to approximately its present length and gave it its received title. In this revision he stripped it of most of the vestiges of its epistolary character, but the recurrent term of address remains: the two-syllable space formerly occupied by *Sara, Wordsworth,* and *William* is here filled by *Edmund*.[10] The space could just as well have been filled, at an early stage when he was bemused between Poole and Wordsworth (or between Poole and Sara), by *Thomas.* And in the received text, based on the 1817 *Sibylline Leaves* version, the space is filled by *lady.* Why *lady*? Coleridge's process of identifying the object of his emotions had come full circle. Why not a masculine referent of two syllables?

ii

Coleridge's uncertainty about the ultimate object of the emotions expressed in *Dejection* resembles a child's inability to separate his feelings for men and his feelings for women. Underlying this confusion is a powerful need to bind the self to another man and the simultaneous impulse to test the bond until it breaks. These needs, only suggested in the history of the composition of the *Dejection* ode, are fully shown in his letters, where he made a series of attempts to create demanding relationships. It may be that

the original *Letter* was composed not as a love letter but rather
as one of those outbursts he inflicted so often on his friends—and
relatives—as a child inflicts them on his parents.

The first of these epistolary attempts (it ought to be remembered that *Dejection* is a letter) is in the letters he wrote to his
brother George beginning in 1791 shortly after he arrived at
Jesus College in Cambridge. He addressed George as "a brother
whose love and care towards me are truly paternal,"[11] as "my
more than brother,"[12] and as "my Brother—my father!"[13] Apparently presupposing a parent's concern for the health of a
child, he recounted the details of his physical condition:

> Indeed I should have written you before, but that
> a bad sore throat and still worse cough prevented
> me from mustering Spirits adequate to the undertaking.
> The sore throat gargarization and attention have
> removed: my cough remains—and is indeed in its
> zenith: not Cerberus ever barked louder: every act of
> tussitation seems to divorce my bowells and belly—
> indeed if the said parties had not a particular
> attachment to one another, they must have been long
> ago separated.[14]

Such explosive physical details[15] persist throughout Coleridge's correspondence with George, which he pursued atten-
tively until the middle of 1794. In February of 1793 he announced to his brother that

> A little more than a fortnight ago a quantity of
> matter chose to form in the socket of a decayed tooth,
> & brought with [it] such violent swelling, inflammation,
> & other parapharnalia [sic] of Pain, as threw me into
> a fever; but, God be praised! my Gum has at last
> been opened, my tooth drawn, and this is the fifth day
> of my convalescence.[16]

James Coleridge, Samuel's eldest surviving brother, was in
Hanson's words, "the head of the family,"[17] but it was always to

George that Coleridge appealed for help of whatever kind. He reported fully to George his progress in Jesus College, he depended on him for money, and occasionally he submitted evidence of his abilities by sending him verses or writing to him in Latin. George was eight years older than Samuel, and it is evident from a letter written from Christ's Hospital in the spring of 1789 that George had by this time begun to assume some of the financial responsibilities that would have belonged to the father who had died in 1781:

> You will excuse me for reminding you that, as our
> Holidays commence next week, and I shall go out a good
> deal, a good pair of breeches will be no inconsiderable
> accession to my appearance.[18]

By the end of 1793, however, Coleridge had put George's "truly paternal" love for him to a severe test. He left Cambridge and without a word to anyone—except "the young men at Christ's Hospital"—[19] enlisted in the cavalry on December 2. After George learned, at third hand,[20] of the enlistment, the letters to the "more than brother" took on an impassioned tone. There is a noticeable need in these letters, written during February and March of 1794, to define himself through confession, self-justification, and self-abasement,[21] apparently in an effort to get understanding, approval, and forgiveness—the equivalent of ideal parental love. It must have been that he feared the withholding of such love, and that he engaged in this kind of self-definition not only in an effort to understand himself but also in order to divert attention from his unconscious hostilities, which would have made him expect punishment.

> What shall I say—what shall [I] write to you?
> Shall I profess an abhorrence of my past conduct? Ah
> me—too well do I know it's Iniquity—but to abhor!
> this feeble & exhausted heart supplies not so strong
> an emotion ... My Brother—my Brother—pray
> for me—comfort me, my Brother! I am very wretched—

and tho' my complaint be bitter, my stroke is heavier
than my groaning.[22]

But by the middle of 1794 Coleridge had seriously impaired
George's perfect love for him, and he began to write intimately
to Southey, whom he met in June of that year on a visit to Oxford.[23] By the time Coleridge was writing to Southey, George
was alarmed not only by the pitiful adventure in the army, which
he had helped Coleridge to terminate, but also by the Pantisocracy scheme. George's anxiety had in fact developed to the point
where he had apparently threatened Samuel with confinement,
remembering perhaps that he had been officially released from
the army on grounds of insanity.[24] At least Coleridge refers to a
confinement in a letter to Southey, which makes it clear that
George has stopped functioning as an ideal image of parental
love:

> There is little danger of my being *confined—Advice*
> offered with *respect* from a *Brother* [George]—
> *affected coldness*, an *assumed alienation*—mixed with
> involuntary bursts of ANGUISH and disappointed
> *Affection*—questions concerning the mode in which
> I would have it [the Pantisocracy scheme] mentioned to
> my aged Mother—these are the daggers, which are
> plunged into *my* Peace![25]

It is equally clear in this letter, which has four months of intimate correspondence with Southey behind it, that Southey is the
new confidant, a replacement for George, another man for whom
Coleridge can define himself through confession, self-justification, and self-abasement. He refers to himself here as a "child of
frailty," he complains about his health ("Ill as I am I must go
out to Supper—"), and he laments the loss of Mary Evans. After
expressing recognition that "I should rather be offering consolation to your sorrows, than be wasting my feelings in egotistic
complaints!" he nevertheless describes his situation with words
that he had already used in a letter to George, a paraphrase from

the book of Job: " 'Verily my Complaint is bitter—yet my Stroke is heavier than my Groaning,' " justifying his "egotistic complaints" at the same time that he rebukes them.

The effort to get understanding, approval, and forgiveness, evident in the letters to George, marks these letters to Southey as well. And the mood in which Coleridge composed his letters to George and Southey might serve equally well as a description of the mood in which he composed the first draft of the *Dejection* ode. Writing to Southey, he confessed that

> I sit down to write to you, not that I have anything
> particular to say—but it is a relief, and forms a very
> respectable part in my theory of Escapes from the folly
> of Melancholy. I am so habituated to philosophizing,
> that I cannot divest myself of it even when my own
> Wretchedness is the subject. I appear to myself like a
> sick Physician, feeling the pang acutely, yet deriving
> a wonted pleasure from examining it's progress and
> developing it's causes.[26]

It is as though he found it impossible to define himself, to validate his identity, except through submission to the glasses of someone else's eyes, like a child, whose only understanding of himself comes to him through parental responses to his behavior. The likelihood is that the examination and development of the progress and causes of his wretchedness were pleasurable not in themselves but rather in their effects on his correspondent, who could be counted on to react and therefore in some sort to judge. The reaction he appeared to want was a loving one; the judgment would then reflect a docile identity for him, the identity of a "good" child.

When the reaction was different from his expectations, Coleridge suffered; Southey's rebukes of his negligent behavior toward Sarah Fricker, for instance, elicited strong responses:

> My fire was blazing chearfully—the Tea-kettle even
> now boiled over on it—how sudden-sad it looks!

but see—it blazes up again as cheerily as ever!—Such,
dear Southey! was the effect of your this morning's
letter on my heart. Angry! no, I esteem & confide in you
the more—: but it *did* make me sorrowful.—I was
blameless—it was therefore only a passing Cloud
empictur'd on the Breast.[27]

The "passing Cloud" re-appeared a few months later:

With regard to neglect respecting——[Sarah],
do you accuse me justly? I have written 5 or 4 letters
since my absence—received one. I am not conscious
of having injured her otherwise, than by having
mistaken the ebullience of *schematism* for affection,
which a moment's reflection might have told me, is not
a plant of so mushroom a growth—had it ever not been
counteracted by a prior attachment/ but my whole
Life has been a series of Blunders! God have mercy
upon me—for I am a most miserable Dog—[28]

He obviously did not feel "blameless" at this point. And a
month later, under increasing criticism from Southey, the suffering grew stronger:

I will not say that you treat me coolly or mysteriously
—yet assuredly you seem to look upon me as a man
whom vanity or some other inexplicable Cause have
alienated from the System [Pantisocracy]—on what
could you have built so injurious a suspicion?—
Wherein when roused to the recollection of my Duty
have I shrunk from the performance of it?—I hold my
Life & my feebler feelings as ready sacrifices to
Justice—Καυχάω ὑπορᾷς[ὑφορᾷς?] γαρ.[29]
I dismiss a subject so painful to me as self-vindication—
painful to me only as addressing it to *you* on whose
esteem and affection I have rested with the whole
weight of my soul.[30]

Now, it appears, it was Southey not George who plunged
daggers into his peace. Like George before him, Southey early in

1795 began to lose his value for Coleridge as an image of parental love, and for a similar reason: he had been subjected to a test that was too difficult. George had failed to survive with loving equanimity Coleridge's flight from Cambridge into the cavalry and his subsequent enthusiasm for a Pantisocratic society in America. But Coleridge set an even more difficult test for Southey. Between 1794 and 1795 he saturated Southey with the whole flood of his ambivalent feelings[31] for Mary Evans and for Sarah Fricker, to whose sister Southey was engaged to be married. Conflicting loyalties undoubtedly led Southey toward a cooler view of his friend, particularly when Coleridge responded badly to Southey's pressure on him in behalf of Sarah. Like George, Southey no longer qualified for the role of understanding, approving, and forgiving confidant. Coleridge rebuked Southey for his failure to meet the test:

> *Love* is an active and humble Principle—It flies not
> away from the Couches of Imperfection, because
> the Patients are fretful or loathsome.[32]

Fretful Coleridge certainly could be, and apparently he felt loathsome as well. And yet, in spite of his plea for perfect love which "flies not away from the Couches of Imperfection" he engaged in the kind of behavior best calculated to lose anybody's love. In both cases—his relationship with George and his relationship with Southey—he deliberately created strains that were too difficult to bear, made emotional demands that were impossible to meet. This sort of conduct, while it undoubtedly caused severe distress to both George and Southey, also had the effect of losing for Coleridge, one after the other, two men "on whose esteem and affection [he had] rested with the whole weight of [his] soul." Although he appeared to be begging for love, he was in fact asking for punishment.

Coleridge's farewell letter to Southey, which fills ten printed pages, is dated November 13, 1795,[33] the day before Southey's marriage to Edith Fricker. Coleridge and Southey had already been alienated from each other for some time,[34] but Coleridge was not moved to compose this long and passionate document of love and hate until the eve of Southey's wedding. The wedding was apparently "secret;"[35] Coleridge did not know how well timed his letter was, any more than he could have known that the *Dejection* ode, a farewell of a different sort, would be published on the morning of Wordsworth's wedding. But Southey's commitment to Edith, like Wordsworth's later commitment to Mary Hutchinson, had been an open matter of long standing. As an inadvertent and inappropriate wedding gift, the letter to Southey compares with the *Dejection* ode. At one level this letter expresses a feeling of abandonment in favor of something or someone else, and it has the force of the uninvited bad fairy's curse at the birthday festivities of Briar Rose. Ostensibly, Coleridge was castigating Southey for his defection from Pantisocracy, his "hypocritical" if temporary idea of entering the church, and in general for behavior that had been at odds with the aspirations he had professed earlier. But some of the sexual imagery suggests that it was the thought of Southey's intimacy with a woman that was intolerable and disgusting:

> . . . Heaven forbid, that I should not now have faith,
> that however foul your Stream may run here, yet
> that it will filtrate & become pure in it's subterraneous
> Passage to the Ocean of Universal Redemption[36] . . .
>   O God! that *such a mind* should fall in love
> with that low, dirty, gutter-grubbing Trull,
> WORLDLY PRUDENCE!!
>   Curse on all *Pride*! 'Tis a Harlot that buckrams
> herself up in Virtue only that she may fetch a
> higher Price.[37]

The full weight of the curse, as prophecy of Southey's sterility, can be felt in the final definition of "Pride" that immediately follows:

'Tis a Rock, where Virtue may be planted but cannot
strike Root.[38]

There is some material, further along in this letter, that
prompts the supposition that Coleridge's confidences to Southey
concerning his ambivalent feelings for Mary Evans and for Sarah
Fricker were an indirect expression of his feelings for Southey
himself:

You have left a large Void in my Heart—I know no
man big enough to fill it. Others I may love equally
& esteem equally: and some perhaps I may admire
as much. But never do I expect to meet another man,
who will make me unite attachment for his person
with reverence for his heart and admiration of his
Genius! I did not only venerate you for your own Virtues,
I prized you as the Sheet Anchor of mine! And even
[as] a Poet, my Vanity knew no keener gratification
than your Praise—But these things are past by, like as
when an hungry man dreams, and lo! he feasteth—
but he awakes, and his Soul is empty![39]

Such intensity of feeling must have been at least one of the
impossible emotional demands which Coleridge levied upon
Southey and under which the friendship broke. This long farewell letter, full of disappointed love and of bitter reproach and
execration, is the climax of a correspondence that illustrates the
range of Coleridge's conflicting emotions—of love and hate—
toward other men even more fully than the letters to George do.
The reason is probably that George inherited, along with financial responsibility, that aspect of their father which prohibited
Coleridge's open expression of anger. As a brother George was
protected, to a degree, from the aggressions that Coleridge could
more safely release toward Southey.

iii

Early in 1796 Coleridge began to write with great intimacy to
Thomas Poole, and by 1797 the letters to Poole show that for

the third time he was trying to find perfect love in another man
and trying also to define himself through the other man's perception of him. This time he chose the method of autobiography:

> ... what I am depends on what I have been; and you,
> MY BEST FRIEND! have a right to the narration.—
> To me the task will be a useful one; it will renew and
> deepen my reflections on the past; and it will perhaps
> make you behold with no unforgiving or impatient
> eye those weaknesses and defects in my character,
> which so many untoward circumstances have concurred
> to plant there.[40]

The bases for Coleridge's ambivalent relationships with other
men are partially revealed in two of the autobiographical letters
he wrote to Poole. In one he wrote that "My Father was very fond
of me, and I was my mother's darling."[41] In another he gave a
long account of his having run away from home as a child, an
episode which, as he told it, seems one calculated to test with
extreme measures the patience of his parents' love for him. The
episode proceeds from an unreasonable demand upon his
mother; but she met the demand and Coleridge seems dimly
aware of its unreasonableness:

> From October 1779 to Oct. 1781.—I had asked my
> mother one evening to cut my cheese *entire*, so that
> I might toast it: this was no easy matter, it being a
> *crumbly* cheese—My mother however did it.[42]

But someone interfered with his mother's gift of love to him
in the matter of the cheese, and Coleridge's response to this interference was so violent as to suggest that the interferer represented to him someone who seriously threatened his closeness to
her:

> I went into the garden for some thing or other, and
> in the mean time my Brother Frank *minced* my cheese,
> 'to disappoint the favorite'. I returned, saw the
> exploit, and in an agony of passion flew at Frank—

he pretended to have been seriously hurt by my blow,
flung himself on the ground, and there lay with
outstretched limbs—I hung over him moaning & in
great fright—he leaped up, & with a horse-laugh
gave me a severe blow in the face—I seized a knife,
and was running at him, when my Mother came in
& took me by the arm—/ I expected a flogging—&
struggling from her I ran away, to a hill at the bottom
of which the Otter flows—about one mile from Ottery.—
There I stayed; my rage died away; but my obstinacy
vanquished my fears—& taking out a little shilling book
which had, at the end, morning & evening prayers,
I very devoutly repeated them—thinking *at the
same time* with inward and gloomy satisfaction, how
miserable my Mother must be![43]

The letter continues, detailing the events of that night when
he eventually fell asleep and "rolled to within three yards of the
River, which flowed by the unfenced edge of the bottom . . .
there I might have lain & died."[44] His parents, he tells Poole,
suffered a sleepless night in his absence, the crier was sent out to
shout for him, "—indeed, I believe, half the town were up all one
night!"[45] When he was finally found and delivered to his parents,
he was met with love:

I remember, & shall never forget, my father's face
as he looked upon me while I lay in the servant's arms—
so calm, and the tears stealing down his face: for I
was the child of his old age.—My Mother, as you may
suppose, was outrageous with joy.[46]

It is difficult to imagine what stronger course he could have
taken—short of having "there . . . lain & died"—to cause pain
to his parents and especially his mother of whom he was "thinking *at the same time*" that he repeated his prayers—in an effort
to prove himself a "good" child—"with inward & gloomy satisfaction, how miserable [she] must be!" This runaway episode
suggests the lengths to which his aggressions drove him, and il-

luminates to some degree the destructive feelings that must have been latent in his later testing of the love of George and of Southey.

His parents' love for him apparently survived this sort of trial with a composure that George and Southey were incapable of; but there was someone, only slightly involved in the situation, who at the time expressed feelings that Coleridge probably excited later in George and in Southey:

> —in rushed a *young Lady*, crying out—'I hope, you'll whip him, Mrs. Coleridge!'[47]

In order to understand more fully the nature of the aggressions that underlay both the runaway episode and his later relationships with other men it will be worthwhile to return to the earlier letter to Poole, which begins, "My Father was very fond of me, and I was my mother's darling." The letter continues:

> —in consequence, I was very miserable. For Molly, who had nursed my brother Francis, and was immoderately fond of him, hated me because my mother took more notice of me than of Frank—and Frank hated me, because my mother gave me now & then a bit of cake, when he had none—quite forgetting that for one bit of cake which I had & he had not, he had twenty sops in the pan & pieces of bread & butter with sugar on them from Molly, from whom I received only thumps and ill names.[48]

This is the context from which Chambers abstracts a single phrase and wonders

> how De Quincey came to think that Samuel had been 'almost an object of persecution to his mother'. It is true that in 1804 Coleridge, who was always inclined to see himself in a dramatic light, wrote to Sir George Beaumont, 'I was hardly used from infancy to boyhood, and from boyhood to youth most, MOST cruelly'. But it is clear from his narratives to Poole and

Gillman that, in so far as this refers to his nursery
rather than his school days, it was not upon his parents
that he laid any blame. 'My father was very fond of
me, and I was my mother's darling: in consequence
I was very miserable.' The trouble was with a nurse
Molly, who was jealous for his next brother Frank,
of whom she made a pet at Samuel's expense.[49]

Chambers has been persuaded by the device with which Coleridge attempted to deceive himself. It was dangerous to be aware
of open hatred toward his mother—almost as dangerous as it
would be to be aware of the nature of his love for her; the fear of
retaliation in the one case and of tabu in the other must have
been powerful deterrents to recognition. Molly, in the image of
the mother, was a convenient figure on whom to displace hatred.
Similarly Frank, drawn into this drama of distortion and displaced feelings, became a scapegoat for the father.

Seen in this triangular light, with Molly at the apex repre-
senting the mother, the rivalry with Frank over cakes and sops in
the pan, and the rage with which Coleridge reacted to Frank's
interference with his mother's gift of love to him, become com-
prehensible. If it was the mother's love that was at stake, then
beneath the apparent sibling rivalry for creature comfort was the
real rivalry with the father. Molly was acting the role of the
"bad" mother who would not give herself to her son; and unfortunately for Frank she acted it so completely as to give more to
him than to Samuel. It is no wonder then that after running at
Frank with a knife Coleridge "expected a flogging" and that his
thoughts turned toward death ("there I might have lain & died").
Frank's retaliatory blow rounds out the drama neatly, supplying
the paternal *coup de grace*; it fully qualifies him for his role opposite Molly as the "bad" father who would punish his son for
attempting to usurp his place.

Molly's role as the "bad" mother explains Coleridge's "inward
and gloomy satisfaction" while he thinks of "how miserable my

Mother must be!" Running away from home, he was not punishing his mother for her overt behavior toward him; after all, she did slice the cheese as he wanted her to and he was, in his own words, "my mother's darling." He was punishing that aspect of her which he did not dare to be aware of, that aspect which was represented by Molly who, withholding favors, symbolized the mother who withholds favors unmentionable and secretly desired. When his mother took him by the arm, presumably to prevent his finishing off Frank with a knife, her image merged, for the moment, with the image of the "bad" mother who not only withholds favors but also punishes the son for attempting to replace the father. This is the mother image Coleridge probably drew for De Quincey, who then was able to believe that Samuel had been "almost an object of persecution to his mother."

Frank's role as the "bad" father, threatened and threatening, is a signal that although Coleridge was consciously aware of his wish to punish his mother ("thinking . . . with inward and gloomy satisfaction how miserable [she] must be"), that awareness was a screen for his unconscious feelings of aggression toward his father. The most dangerous wish of all was his wish to destroy the father in order to become the father.

It produced in Coleridge a persistent need to represent himself as a "child of frailty"[50] who could not possibly be suspected of anger or of destructive feelings.[51] His recurrent claims to frailty indicate, among other things, that there was very little distance between the point of view of the man who wrote to Poole and the point of view of the child he once had been. Having finished off the account of his runaway episode with the cry of the *"young Lady"*—"I hope, you'll whip him, Mrs. Coleridge!"—he continued in the letter to show that old rancors persisted almost unmitigated by time, although they were displaced from their original objects:

> This woman still lives at Ottery—& neither Philosophy
> or Religion have been able to conquer the antipathy

which I *feel* towards her, whenever I see her.—I was
put to bed—& recovered in a day or so—but I was
certainly injured—For I was weakly, & subject to
the ague for many years after—.[52]

The grown man was still persuaded that someone or something
had intolerably abused him, the recollected suggestion that he
should not escape whipping moved in him the old, durable fury,
and in an attempt to deny his aggressive part in the episode he
accounted for his recurrent respiratory ailments by means of his
exposure on that occasion.

A similar lack of distance between the mature and the imma-
ture points of view is shown in the earlier letter to Poole explaining the triangular situation with Molly and Frank, where, years
later, he had still not forgiven Molly and, what is more important, he was still concerned to show that in this *mélange* of tan-
gled rivalries Frank had come off better than he had. The detail
with which he remembered the "sops in the pan & pieces of bread
& butter with sugar on them" is curiously and childishly hungry.
The child of frailty—abused, sickly, and deprived—forever.
Who could suspect him of murderous self-assertion?

Immediately after the account of the runaway episode in the
letter to Poole, Coleridge, in what seems to be an attempt to push
down and deny these dangerously destructive feelings toward his
father, turned to a long panegyric which details some extremely
pleasurable aspects of companionship with him, as though in an
effort to prove not only that his father was lovable but also that
he had in fact loved not hated him. And in the final passage of
the letter he related the circumstances of his father's death in
such a way as to provide fair certainty of the guilt which these
feelings aroused in him:

Towards the latter end of September 1781 my Father
went to Plymouth with my Brother Francis, who was
to go as Midshipman under Admiral Graves; the Admiral
was a friend of my Father's.—My Father settled my

Brother; & returned Oct. 4th, 1781—. He arrived
at Exeter about six o'clock—& was pressed to take a bed
there by the Harts—but he refused—and to avoid
their intreaties he told them—that he had never been
superstitious—but that the night before he had had
a dream which had made a deep impression. He dreamt
that Death had appeared to him, as he is commonly
painted, & touched him with his Dart. Well he returned
home—& all his family, I excepted, were up. He told
my mother his dream—; but he was in high health &
good spirits—& there was a bowl of Punch made—
& my Father gave a long & particular account of his
Travel, and that he had placed Frank under a religious
Captain &c—/ At length, he went to bed, very well,
& in high Spirits.—A short time after he had lain down
he complained of a pain in his bowells, which he was
subject to, from the wind—my mother got him some
peppermint water—and after a pause, he said—'I am
much better now, my dear!'—and lay down again.
In a minute my mother heard a noise in his throat—
and spoke to him—but he did not answer—and she
spoke to him—but he did not answer—and she spoke
repeatedly in vain. Her *shriek* awaked me—&
I said, 'Papa is dead.'—I did not know [of] my Father's
return, but I knew that he was expected. How I came
to think of his Death, I cannot tell; but so it was.—
Dead he was.[53]

How his father came to dream of his death we shall never
know; but we may speculate that how Samuel came to think of
it was that it was a fearful wish fearfully expressed and that it
had its terrifying and guilt-inspiring fulfillment. It appears from
Coleridge's juxtaposition of both events in one letter that he unconsciously felt a causal relationship between the aggressions
that impelled him to run away from home and the fact of his father's death. He associated the two events again for Gillman:

> I forget whether it was in my fifth or sixth year, but I
> believe the latter, in consequence of some quarrel
> between me and my brother, in the first week of October,
> I ran away from fear of being whipped, and passed
> the whole night, a night of rain and storm, on the bleak
> side of a hill on the Otter, and was found there at day-
> break, without the power of using my limbs, about six
> yards from the naked bank of the river.
>   In my seventh year, about the same time, if not the
> very same time, i.e. Oct. 4th, my most dear, most revered
> father, died suddenly.[54]

Apparently there was a close connection in his mind—the kind
of magical connection children make—between his quarrel with
Frank and his father's death. Running at Frank with a knife, he
was asserting the full strength of his destructive impulses against
his father. The seasonal coincidence of his father's death ("about
the same time [as the runaway episode], if not the very same
time") with this violent assertion of Coleridge's wish to usurp his
place must have served to reinforce the connection and to convince him emotionally of his guilty part in that death.

Coleridge's central nostalgia was toward his mother and his
central anger was toward his father, and both these feelings were
so dangerous that he had to disguise if not deny them. Their earliest disguise was apparently accomplished through their displacement on to Molly and Frank.

By the time he wrote the *Dejection* ode, his oedipal tensions
had so complicated his sexual responses that he could not choose
between a male and a female love object. His vacillation among
various referents in the versions of the poem reflects what must
have been his childhood vacillation as he tried to lessen the dangers of attaching his passionate feelings to his parents.

iv

As it turned out, Coleridge's displacement of his feelings for his
father on to his brother Frank, instead of helping him to avoid

oedipal punishment, appears to have strengthened his need for such punishment. Frank was two years older than Samuel; he was born in 1770, in the same year with Wordsworth. Coleridge's first reference to him in a letter to Poole is an admiring one:

> —All my Brothers are remarkably handsome; but
> they were as inferior to Francis as I am to them. He went
> by the name of 'the handsome Coleridge.'[55]

But his next reference—in a letter that precedes the one in which he recounts his runaway experience—appears to express strong feelings of both love and hate on both sides:

> —I had a dangerous putrid fever this year [1778-
> 1779]—My Brother George lay ill of the same fever
> in the next room.—My poor Brother Francis, I
> remember, stole up in spite of orders to the contrary,
> & sate by my bedside, & read Pope's Homer to me—
> Frank had a violent love of beating me—but whenever
> that was superseded by any humour or circumstance,
> he was always very fond of me—& used to regard me
> with a strange mixture of admiration & contempt—
> strange it was not—: for he hated books, and loved
> climbing, fighting, playing, & robbing orchards, to
> distraction.[56]

Frank lived to be only twenty-two years old. Having enlisted in the navy a few days before their father died,[57] he obtained a commission through the intervention of his elder brother John. On February 6, 1792, after the fall of Seringapatam, he shot himself and died. Coleridge did not get the news of Frank's death until early in 1793—about a year after the event. His acknowledgment of it is dropped almost casually into a letter to George— the letter that begins with the description of his "decayed tooth." He gets around to Frank in the third paragraph:

> —Poor Francis! I have shed the tear of natural affection
> over him.—He was the only one of my Family, whom

> similarity of Ages made more peculiarly my Brother—
> he was the hero of all the little tales, that make the
> remembrance of my earliest days interesting!—Yet
> his Death filled me rather with Melancholy than
> Anguish.[58]

Apparently he was aware of a special relationship between him and Frank and he was—consciously at least—mildly surprised that Frank's death should cause him no real "Anguish." He accounted for his feeling failure by his having "quitted Ottery, when I was so young,"[59] and by the fact that for him childhood was associated not with his family and his birthplace but with Christ's Hospital. It is likelier, however, that he was less unable than unwilling to feel strongly about Frank's death. Unconscious magical connections were perhaps again at work in his mind: the murderous fantasies—abortively acted out in his attack on Frank with a knife—that "caused" his father's death were stirred again and the resultant guilt was reinforced by Frank's death which those fantasies might also have "caused."

If Frank existed for Coleridge as the father, that role was solidified by their unity, so to speak, produced by death. It is significant that Coleridge's attempt to create a filial relationship with his brother George began to break down in the year when he heard of Frank's suicide. The stirring of guilt creates the need for punishment, and Coleridge's behavior during the latter part of 1793 and the early part of 1794 appears to express profound guilt and a need for the ultimate form of punishment. The "Anguish" he failed to feel consciously for Frank's death was perhaps so strenuously submerged that there was very little energy left over from the effort, and he fell into a severe depression.

Coleridge's ability to withstand the news of Frank's death, which had reached him at Cambridge by February of 1793, was considerably weakened in two important ways. He had just failed to win a university scholarship in competition with three other students,[60] and he had been separated for almost a year from his

friend Thomas Fanshawe Middleton, who had left Cambridge
because he had failed to get a university fellowship. The association of Frank's death and Middleton's departure is made by
Chambers in a narration of the early part of 1793:

> His letters to the Evans family are in the old vein,
> but less cheerful. He has lost his brother Frank and a
> friend, probably Middleton.[61]

Chambers evidently based his association of these two events on
a letter to Anne Evans dated February 10, 1793, in which Coleridge wrote that "within this last month I have lost a Brother and
a Friend! But I struggle for chearfulness."[62] But Coleridge had
not "lost" Middleton "within this last month;" Middleton's departure from Cambridge was already almost a year in the past.
There is a chance that the letter to Anne Evans demonstrates
Coleridge's characteristic refusal to come to terms with time[63]
and that Chambers has been infected with Coleridge's associa-
tional habits of thought.

There is some evidence that Middleton was for Coleridge a
figure "like" Frank. At least Gillman's narrative shows Middleton to have been paternally protective and an object both of admiration and of rivalry:

> Coleridge's own account is, that while Middleton,
> afterwards Bishop of Calcutta, remained at Pembroke
> [in Cambridge], he "worked with him and was
> industrious, read hard, and obtained the prize for the
> Greek Ode," &c[64] ... After Middleton's departure,
> the keen desire which Coleridge previously felt for the
> possession of honours abated, and he became indifferent
> to them[65] ... Middleton, loving Coleridge so much,
> and being his senior in years, as well as in studies, was
> to him, while at school and at college, what the Polar
> Star is to the mariner on a wide sea without compass,—
> his guide, and his influential friend and companion[66] ...
> At the departure of Middleton, to whom he always

looked up, whose success he had considered morally
certain, and whose unexpected failure was therefore the
more painful to his feelings, he became desponding,
and, in addition, vexed and fretted by college debts,
he was overtaken by that inward grief, the product
of fear, which he, in after life, so painfully described
in his Ode to Dejection.[67]

The relationship with Middleton must have been another of
Coleridge's efforts to bind himself in a filial tie, and its rivalrous
character partly explains Coleridge's strong sense of academic
inadequacy, apparently unjustified,[68] which had colored his two
years in Cambridge, as well as the indolence into which he fell
after Middleton's failure. The rivalry was dangerous, and his rival's failure could have been magically attributed to his own
efforts to surpass him, so that "indolence" could have set in as a
denial of self-assertion. It is interesting that Gillman attributes
Coleridge's "inward grief" to "fear," which should be interpreted
as fear of retaliation—a powerful deterrent, for Coleridge, to
any contest.

Frank's death then was an event to cap the loss of Middleton,
and it is not surprising that Coleridge might have associated the
two, although evidence that he did so is pretty cloudy. But there
is no doubt about the "desponding" character of this period. In
addition to Coleridge's academic disappointment (or retreat from
effort), a series of debts was quite realistically piling up about
him.[69] He spent the summer in Ottery, and by August 5 he was
writing to George in severe distress, imagining (perhaps cor-
rectly) that George's failure to write to him was a sign of displeas-
ure over his erratic behavior with money.[70]

Between August 5, 1793, and February 6, 1794, there is only
one letter from Coleridge—a short note to the editor of the
Morning Chronicle[71] enclosing a poem with the title *To For-
tune, On buying a Ticket in the Irish Lottery.* The poem was published on November 7, 1793,[72] but he did not win the lottery.

For six months, apparently, his depression took the form of a withdrawal, broken only by the impulse to try his luck—or perhaps to prove to himself his bad luck.

Ten months after Coleridge got word of Frank's suicide in the navy, he himself enlisted in the army, on December 2, 1793, secretly and under an assumed name. This move has been interpreted as a desperate attempt to escape from his debts or from his unhappy love for Mary Evans;[73] but his own account of the mood that preceded his enlistment seems to argue for an alternative view. On February 23, 1794, while his brothers George and James were attempting to get his military discharge, he wrote to George a lengthy letter of self-reproach, full of confession and penitence, prefaced however with a disarming statement about his ill health:

> My Brother would have heard from me long ere this,
> had I not been unwell—unwell indeed—I verily
> thought, that I was hastening to that quiet Bourne,
> Where grief is hush'd—And when my recovered
> Strength would have permitted me to have written to
> you, so utterly dejected were my Spirits, that my letter
> would have displayed such a hopelessness of all future
> Comfort, as would have approached to Ingratitude.[74]

Having fully established himself as a harmless "child of frailty," he proceeds to catalog his vices: laziness, cowardice, furtiveness, intemperance, and so on and on. From the letter it is apparent that George and James, finally made aware of Coleridge's college debts, had given him the money to settle them but that he had frittered almost all of it away without paying his creditors. The result was that

> My agitations were delirium . . . On Sunday night
> I packed up a few things,—went off in the mail —
> staid about a week in a strange way, still looking
> forwards with a kind of recklessness to the dernier
> resort of misery—An accident of a very singular kind

prevented me—and led me to adopt my present situation.[75]

"Looking forwards . . . to the dernier resort of misery" certainly means that Coleridge was contemplating suicide, the "resort" which Frank had chosen. There is no available light on the "accident" that made Coleridge choose military anonymity instead, but this choice is in important ways strikingly similar to the other choice, of suicide, especially in view of his assertion to George in a letter from the military camp that he wishes he were dead: "O that the shadow of Death were on my Eyelids!"[76] If, as I am assuming, the various events of his life at this time combined to produce a crescendo of guilt and self-disgust which only extreme punishment could appease, his life in the army—however brief—surely provided the punishment next best to death:

> . . . my present situation—where what I have suffered
> —but enough—may he, who in mercy dispenseth
> Anguish, be gracious to me.[77]

The secrecy with which he enlisted and the signing of his name as Silas Tomkyn Comberbache reflect a profound wish not to be. It is noteworthy that this experience afforded him—"in mercy"—that "Anguish" which he told George he did not feel when he heard the news of Frank's death. And his enlistment *in the army*, after failing to die as Frank died, appears to express his need for a type of punishment which would be "like" Frank's death. Vengeance for his murderous feelings toward Frank— because they masked murderous feelings toward his father— required the equivalent of an eye for an eye.

This episode in Coleridge's life appears to contain all the elements of a full-blown period of dejection—a sense of loss (referred to as "suffering"), heightened guilt feelings in the face of "magical" results of his aggressive fantasies, the effort to deny these fantasies by means of the device of assuming the character of a "child of frailty" (suffering again), and the longing for death

as punishment (expressed in his withdrawal from life into the
army under an assumed name)—a kind of rehearsal for the great
dejection period that took place in 1802, when he composed *A
Letter to*——. But if his feelings of guilt at this time appear to
foreshadow the feelings that were to emerge in 1802, they also
recall the feelings that must have been aroused in him years earlier when his father died.

In one of the autobiographical notes which Coleridge wrote
for Gillman, he observes that

> When I was first plucked up and transplanted from
> my birth place and family, at the death of my dear
> father, whose revered image has ever survived in my
> mind, to make me know what the emotions and
> affections of a son are, and how ill a father's place is
> likely to be supplied by any other relation, Providence
> (it has often occurred to me) gave the first intimation,
> that it was my lot, and that it was best for me, to
> make or find my way of life a detached individual, a
> Terrae Filius.[78]

Despite this providential intimation Coleridge continued, as
we have seen, to try to create a "relation" which would supply
his father's place long after the time when he "was first plucked
up and transplanted . . . at the death of [his] dear father." Perhaps his unconscious impulse toward destroying these relationships reflected a need to believe that a father was irreplaceable
and that he was destined to remain "a detached individual, a
Terrae Filius," although these phrases ring more with self-pity
than with accurate self-analysis. The death of his father deprived
him of the opportunity—if there could have been one—to resolve his oedipal tensions; it also apparently surprised his guilt
sufficiently so that he found it recurrently necessary to lick the
resultant wound in a series of abortive attempts to resolve those
tensions in quasi-homoerotic relationships with other men. The
loss of the father at so early an age also produced an emotional

stasis, so that the nature of his particular form of oedipal tension, which he carried all his life, was essentially infantile: the desire for the mother was confused between sexual and oral needs, as it is in the very young child who cannot sort out the various forms of pleasure that are established at the mother's breast.

Coleridge was not quite nine years old when his father died; and he was less than ten years old when in 1782 he lost his mother as a result of his being sent to school at Christ's Hospital. He was indeed "too soon transplanted, ere [his] soul had fixed its first domestic loves;"[79] so that he was ill suited to the role of "a detached individual, a Terrae Filius." His efforts to create filial relationships, to replace his father with another man against whom he could measure and define himself, and from whom he could receive understanding, approval, and forgiveness (in short, ideal parental love), appear to have been made in order to deny the operation of magical causality between his fantasies and his father's death and in effect to deny that his father had died at all. His impulse to destroy such relationships, to receive from another man the punishment he felt he deserved as a result of his unconscious destructive fantasies, permitted him to relive masochistically the loss of his father. But Frank's death forced him to relive that experience too vividly, and it stirred a stronger need—the need for the ultimate punishment: death.

3. Alhadra and Other Mothers

When angry with——, reflect how she would weep
& be in anguish over my death-pillow, & how she
would never forget me?—Coleridge

i

Coleridge's mother took her place with all the death-dealing De-
lilahs, created in the unconscious fantasies of sons and lovers to
seduce and betray, in the moment when she prevented him from
symbolically destroying his father as he was literally going after
his brother Francis with a knife. In that same moment, apparently, she took her place also as symbolic progenitor of all the
other women with whom Coleridge attempted to form attach-
ments. It seems clear that the unconscious connections he made
between his mother and other women contributed to what he
called his dejection, and it is interesting to see how these connections are expressed in his life and in his work.

A consideration of Coleridge *vis-à-vis* women reveals a dramatic situation in which there are three personae: Coleridge the
child, Coleridge the man either remembering or reenacting
childhood, and Coleridge the poet elaborating[1] the emotional experience of childhood in his art. For the most part, these three
personae tend to overlap, or to mingle their points of view; occasionally they conflict and separate in order to deny each other.

It is too easy therefore to label Coleridge's efforts to define
himself as deliberate self-revelation. Certainly there is an element of exhibitionism in his art and in his letters, particularly
the letters to Southey; besides its signal toward latent voyeurism,[2]
in its confessional aspect it functions as a disguise for hostility.

34

In fact, most of what looks like self-revelation in Coleridge is an effort to disguise himself. The primitive emotions, which the child attempted to deny by means of saying his prayers, and which the man could express to George, Southey, and Poole only partially and with the disguises of frailty and love, are not fully released even in his art.

He began to elaborate autobiography in his art while he was writing his autobiographical letters to Poole. On February 6, 1797, he wrote two letters. One was to Richard Brinsley Sheridan:

> I received a letter last Saturday from a friend of the
> Revd W. L. Bowles, importing that *You* wished me
> 'to write a tragedy on some popular subject.' I need not
> say, that I was gratified and somewhat elated by the
> proposal; and whatever hours I can win from the
> avocations, by which I earn my immediate subsistence,
> shall be sacred to the attempt.[3]

The other letter written on this date was addressed to Poole and announced Coleridge's intention to "relate the events of his own Life." On a Sunday in March he gave him an account of his brothers, including the death of Frank and his eulogy of "the handsome Coleridge." And it was in March that he began work (at Stowey, where he had taken a house to be near Poole)[4] on his tragedy *Osorio*. By October 14, it was completed.[5]

On October 16, then, the date on which he wrote for Poole the account of his runaway experience and of his father's death, he had finished writing *Osorio*. In fact he sent a transcript of the play to Bowles on the same day, with instructions to deliver it to Sheridan.[6] The promptness with which he began work on *Osorio* suggests that he had already begun to think of a subject when he wrote the letter to Sheridan on February 6, and his arguments in the letter in favor of a "fictitious and domestic subject" rather than "one founded on well-known History" support the suggestion. It is likely then that the subject of the tragedy stimulated his letters to Poole, just as some of his later poetry can be seen to stimulate his dreams about childhood.[7]

Many of the childhood attitudes that have already been considered are present in *Osorio*, and the *dramatis personae* have the shifting character of figures in a dream-work; Coleridge's artistic elaborations in this drama are not very complex. The chief character is Osorio, who has hired an assassin, Ferdinand, to murder his elder brother Albert so that he can court and marry Albert's fiancee Maria. In order to account for Albert's death, Osorio has told Maria and his father Velez that he saw Albert die on a ship at sea (Frank died while he was in the navy) in an encounter with a pirate ship. So far the narrative seems to represent the conflict between Coleridge and his brother Frank over feminine favors, with the father vaguely in the background. Like Coleridge, Osorio has not himself killed his elder brother; his action in arranging for his death corresponds with Coleridge's destructive fantasies about Frank. Just as Frank symbolizes the father, the presence of Velez points to a symbolic equation in the play between the father and the elder brother Albert.[8]

There are some complications. In the first place, there are two fathers in the play: one is Velez, father of the brothers, who urges Maria to accept Osorio's suit despite her aversion to him and her faithfulness to Albert; and the other is the father of Alhadra's children, Ferdinand the assassin, whom Osorio, out of fear that Ferdinand will betray his secret, murders. Thus we have, in a relatively simple disguise, the "good" father who loves the younger son and the "bad" father who threatens him and who therefore has to be destroyed.

It is Alhadra who avenges her husband's death by ordering Osorio to be killed. Like Coleridge's own "bad" mother, she punishes the usurping son with death. Just as the father image in the play is split into the "good" and "bad" fathers who represent respectively Coleridge's conscious and unconscious feelings for his father, so the mother image is also split into the "bad" Alhadra who is the agent of Osorio's punishment by death and the "good" Maria who is desirable and unattainable.

Maria's unattainable quality rather weights the balance in the play in favor of the "bad" mother, since withholding favors is a characteristic of the "bad" mother. And her nature is further complicated by the fact that she is an orphan whose parents bestowed her in infancy on Velez. Explaining her unwillingness to be courted by Osorio and her faithfulness to Albert, she refers to her closeness to the elder brother:

> ... Were we not
> Born on one day, like twins of the same parent?[9]

This looks superficially like the characteristic Romantic disguise of the incest theme, and in a way it is. But the twinning of Maria with Albert suggests less a narcissistically incestuous relationship between them—or between Maria and Osorio—than it does a confusion in the poet's mind about the object of his erotic emotions. Osorio feels the same ambivalence toward Albert that Coleridge expressed in his letters about Frank. Hearing Ferdinand's story about his encounter with Albert, Osorio is overcome by remorse and recalls Coleridge's reference to "the handsome Coleridge:"

> ... And you kill'd him?
> O blood-hounds! may eternal wrath flame round you!
> He was the image of the Deity.[10]

The confusion between Coleridge's feelings for men and his feelings for women, expressed in the history of the composition of the *Dejection* ode, and suggested in his correspondence with Southey, is reiterated here: Maria is "like" a sister, but she is also "like" a brother. Osorio "loves" her, but the passion that motivates the play is his "love" for Albert—the "love" that generates remorse.[11] It resembles his "love" for Southey.

In his preface to the manuscript he sent to Sheridan, Coleridge calls attention to a number of what he refers to as "great defects" in it. Among them he finds that

Worse than all, the growth of Osorio's character is
nowhere explained—and yet I had most clear and
psychologically accurate ideas of the whole of it . . . A
man, who from constitutional calmness of appetites,
is seduced into pride and the love of power, by these
into misanthropism, or rather a contempt of mankind,
and from thence, by the co-operation of envy, and a
curiously modified love for a beautiful female (which
is nowhere developed in the play), into a most atrocious
guilt.[12]

Two references in this passage deserve attention. One is to the
"most atrocious guilt." This may point to the attempted fratricide
in the play, but the attempt is abortive and Albert survives, fulfilling Coleridge's wish to deny both Frank's and his father's
death. The murder that is accomplished in the play is Osorio's
murder of Ferdinand the "bad" father, and it is for this that
Osorio dies, fulfilling Coleridge's need for the ultimate punishment. Like Wordsworth's drama *The Borderers*, which was written at about the same time, *Osorio* represents the murder of a
father in a curiously ambiguous way. The elaboration is more
complex in *The Borderers* than it is in *Osorio*: not only does
Marmaduke not murder his own father (Herbert is referred to
in the play as a "mock father"[13] and he is the father of the woman
Marmaduke loves) but also he does not "really" murder this father substitute at all. There is less ambiguity in *Osorio* where
there is no doubt either of Osorio's crime or of the punishment
he receives for it. The other striking reference in the preface is to
"a curiously modified love for a beautiful female (which is nowhere developed in the play)." Apparently Coleridge recognized
that Osorio's feeling for Maria is not "real" love, but whether he
made a connection in his mind between this "curiously modified
love" and the fact that he was not able to present it fully and
convincingly in the play is a question.

ii

No matter how darkly and through what glass you look at Coleridge it is evident that there was something "wrong" in his relationships with women. Marshall Suther, in *The Dark Night of Samuel Taylor Coleridge,* is one of three recent critics to take up the problem of Coleridge's attitudes toward women.[14] Leaving aside Suther's thesis, which is that Coleridge's lifelong need for unqualified love was really a religious need, it is worth pointing out that he establishes firmly the idea that Coleridge did not want a sexual relationship.

On the other hand, Suther has been misled into some curious paths of observation:

> Although he speaks of having been spoiled as a child,
> there is little indication that he received much real
> affection, or affection based on any degree of under-
> standing of the kind of creature he was . . . His one
> close emotional attachment in his family seems to have
> been to his sister, who died when he was nineteen.[15]

The evidence for the first of these statements, as it applies to the years before Coleridge was sent away to school, would be difficult to find, in the light of the autobiographical letters to Poole which have already been considered. And it is these years which are commonly referred to as "formative;" at the age of ten, when he entered Christ's Hospital, he had entered the period of emotional latency as well, a period in which the dangerous feelings that had been aroused earlier had to be subdued. It was not lack of parental affection that had stirred these feelings, but the seal of his father's early death upon his oedipal fantasies.

As for the second statement, about Coleridge's sister, Suther sustains it by means of a quotation from the poem "To a Friend" which was written to Charles Lamb in 1794:[16]

> It was to her that he "pour'd forth all [his] puny sorrow
> . . . and of the heart those hidden maladies."[17]

The poem from which he quotes is, in the part which refers to Anne Coleridge, a reworked version of one[18] of two poems Coleridge wrote in 1791 after Anne died. It is an English sonnet, as conventional in its sentiment of mourning as it is in form and diction. In the same year he wrote another sonnet, "On Receiving an Account that his Only Sister's Death was Inevitable," its rhyme scheme a bit more experimental in the combination of English and Italian forms; but it is less concerned with Anne's death than it is with the poet's conviction that he is destined to be a *Terrae Filius*:

> Fated to rove thro' Life's wide cheerless plain—
> Nor father, brother, sister meet its ken—
> My woes, my joys unshared. Ah! long ere then
> On me thy icy dart, stern Death, be prov'd;—
> Better to die, than live and not be lov'd![19]

These two poems provide the only extended references to his sister. The letter to Poole which gives a detailed account of all his brothers does no more than mention her in passing as "the 8th Child . . . [who] died a little after my Brother Luke—aged 21./ Rest, gentle Shade! & wait thy Maker's will;/ Then rise *unchang'd,* and be an Angel still!"[20] This undistinguished conceit immediately precedes the full account of Frank's suicide and the reference to him as "the handsome Coleridge." There appears then to be no evidence for Suther's observation that "the one close emotional attachment in his family seems to have been to his sister."

Of course Coleridge had her age wrong; if she was the eighth child and Francis the ninth, she could not have been twenty-one in 1791, since Francis was twenty-two in 1792 when he died. In fact she was twenty-four. Coleridge made a similar mistake when he told Poole that his brother Luke was twenty-two instead of twenty-five when he died.[21] It is not always easy to account for Coleridge's modifications of the facts of time, but both of these errors seem to proceed from the same source: the powerful impression Frank's suicide made on him, and the subsequent exaggeration of the youthfulness of both his sister and his brother.

The confusion of Anne's age with Frank's also looks like the background for the twinning of Albert and Maria in *Osorio*. Insofar as that twinning was deliberate, it may be simply a device for disguising a narcissistically based incest theme; but while it expresses overtly a nympholeptic quest,[22] like Shelley's, for instance, it expresses ultimately one aspect of Coleridge's primitive quest for his father—that aspect which confused men and women as objects of erotic feeling.

Such confusion may have arisen from a reversal of sexual roles in his family, as one of the letters to Poole suggests:

> My Father (who had so little of parental ambition in
> him, that he had destined his children to be Blacksmiths
> &c, & had accomplished his intention but for my
> Mother's pride & spirit of aggrandizing her family)
> my father had however resolved, that I should be a
> Parson.[23]

Even if Coleridge's contrast between his father's amiable passivity and his mother's aggressiveness is a distortion, the fact would still be that he saw his parents in this light, that he found it necessary to reverse their roles himself.

A notebook entry in the year 1800 supports the possibility of such a confusion in Coleridge's feelings:

> Pleasures of Religion
> Introduction My Mother—prayer in the Lap—prayer
> by the bed side—prayer in the great Hall at evening/
> Church—Cathedral—/ Mother associated with God—
> Father—Schoolmaster—Clergyman—play after school/
> God with rocks &c—[24]

Is the mother here associated with God and the father associated with Schoolmaster—Clergyman—play after school? The associations that are enclosed by slant marks do not permit a ready separation of the sexes. The element of play after school seems to indicate that the separation of mother and father is not intended but that the mother is associated with all the images that follow before the closing slant line.

In her comment on this entry Coburn notes that "The image of the child on the mother's lap is recurrent,"[25] and so it is, in various forms in the verse. But in the letter to Poole which relates the circumstances of his father's death and details the joys of companionship with him, Coleridge presents this image:

> —and my father was fond of me, & used to take me on
> his knee, and hold long conversations with me.[26]

It is just possible that the recurrent image of the child on the mother's lap is an elaboration and that the lap Coleridge longed for was his father's, a reassuring place of comfort where he could deny, by means of affection, his feelings of anger and hostility toward him. It is of course obvious that Coleridge's father was associated for him with religion: he was after all the vicar in Ottery and he did choose Samuel from among all his children to be a parson.

The notebook entry reproduced above seems to reinforce the idea that both the father and the mother are associated to religion and that they are associated also, and confusingly, with each other. Two more entries, dated September 22 and October 12, 1796, clearly show the mother's association to religion and at the same time indicate hesitancy in acknowledging it:

> Speak of my Mother as teaching me to lisp my early
> prayers.[27]
> A word that is clothed about with Death—
> Mother of Love, & Fear, & Holy Hope.[28]

In the first of these entries the word *Mother* is inked over; in the second, the "word" referred to is also *Mother* and is also inked over.

The second of these entries, a paraphrase from the *Apocrypha,* besides the doubt it reveals about the appropriateness of the mother as its dominating figure, more importantly sets some generalized "mother" in a context that seems to be composed of the elements of a *liebestod* theme[29] which recalls the feelings that were present in the account of his runaway experience that he gave to Poole. The heroine is the secretly desired mother who inspires both hope and fear: hope that is "holy" is numinous and carries the implication of tabu, and fear is fear of punishment, in this instance at the hands of the mother, for the crime of usurpation. This "Mother of Love, & Fear, & Holy Hope" prefigures not only the complementary characters of Maria and Alhadra in *Osorio* but the nightmare life-in-death of the *Rime*, Geraldine in *Christabel*, and the Abyssinian maid in *Kubla Khan*[30] as well.

The only primary evidence for the nature of Coleridge's feelings for his mother, aside from his autobiographical letters, is in the one surviving letter he wrote to her on February 4, 1785, from Christ's Hospital, when he was thirteen years old, four years after his father's death and three years after he had been sent away to school. Even allowing for the characteristic taciturnity of children's letters, it can be seen that this one is unusually empty of emotion. It is composed entirely of a catalog of thanks, rigidly itemized with a fine concern for duty and for the value of things:

> Dear Mother,—I received your letter with pleasure on the second instant, and should have had it sooner, but that we had not a holiday before last Tuesday when my brother delivered it to me. I also with gratitude received the two handkerchiefs and the half-a-crown from Mr. Badcock, to whom I would be glad if you gave my thanks. I shall be more careful of the somme [he means that he will in future take better care of his money], as I now consider that were it not for my kind friends I should be as destitute of many little necessaries as some of my schoolfellows are; and Thank God and my relations for them! My brother Luke[31] saw Mr.

James Sorrel, who gave my brother a half-a-crown from
Mrs. Smerdon, but mentioned not a word of the plumb
cake, and said he would call again. Return my most
respectful thanks to Mrs. Smerdon for her kind favour.
My aunt was so kind as to accommodate me with a
box. I suppose my sister Anna's beauty has many
admirers.[32] My brother Luke says that Burke's Art of
Speaking would be of great use to me. If Master Sam
and Harry Badcock are not gone out of [Ottery], give
my kindest love to them. Give my compliments to
Mr. Blake and Miss Atkinson, Mr. and Mrs. Smerdon,
Mr. and Mrs. Clapp, and all other friends in the country.
My uncle, aunt, and cousins join with myself and
Brother in love to my sisters,[33] and hope they are well,
as I, your dutiful son,
                    S. Coleridge, am at present.
P.S. Give my kind love to Molly.[34]

It is noteworthy that he finds no occasion in this letter to thank
his mother for anything, possibly because she has not given him
what he secretly wants; nor does he ask anything of her except
obliquely in his detached and erroneous[35] report of Luke's recom-
mendation of a book, since hope is useless. Both love and hate
are apparently sterilized out of his consciousness here as being
too dangerous. The heavy emphasis on receiving things—including the missing "plumb cake"—is further evidence that Coleridge's desire for his mother was characterized largely by infantile
oral needs.

The postscript, a pathetic afterthought, throws an ironic color
over all the protestations of love and thanks (to everyone except
his mother) that have gone before it: "kind love" he surely does
not feel for the detested Molly, and his offer of it seems to be
made as an incantation to ward off the evil spirit of retaliation.
In fact the whole letter is a kind of incantation which corresponds precisely to the detail, in his account to Poole of his runaway episode, of his repetition of prayers on that occasion "think-

ing *at the same time* with inward and gloomy satisfaction, how miserable my Mother must be!" And the letter serves precisely the same purpose that the prayers served: to prove himself a "good" child.

What emerges from the letter, in spite of its overt docility, is a fairly aggressive self-pity, a mode of feeling that must be what Coleridge later referred to for Gillman's benefit as the providential intimation that "it was best for me to make or find my way of life a detached individual, a Terrae Filius." Just as he persuaded himself that his runaway experience had "certainly injured" him, he is here persuaded that he is almost hopelessly deprived of creature comforts. Of course the Coleridges were poor and there is some reality in his sense of material deprivation; there is reality too in the loneliness and absence of love he must have felt as a child after having been virtually orphaned at the age of ten. The defensive mask of the "child of frailty," tried on in order to protect himself in early childhood, had plenty of stiffening from the later events of his life, and it is no wonder that it congealed permanently on his face.

It certainly must have been reinforced by James Boyer, for instance, headmaster of Christ's Hospital, of whom Campbell writes serenely that "his floggings did his pupil no serious harm that we know of;"[36] and the floggings must also have satisfied— and encouraged—to some extent Coleridge's guilty need for punishment. Early in his schoolboy career, Coleridge received from Boyer a memorable exhortation:

> Boy! the school is your father! Boy! the school is
> your mother! the school is your brother! the school is
> your sister! the school is your first cousin, and your
> second cousin, and all the rest of your relations! Let's
> have no more crying![37]

Boyer's influence can hardly have been benign, particularly since it was operative during the period that followed very soon after the father's death—a period that must necessarily have been

colored by an intensification, through guilt, of the submergence
of love and hate. The spectacle of Boyer, on the occasion of that
exhortation, making himself, *vis-à-vis* the school, the father in-
carnate and destroying at one stroke the validity of all the rest
of Coleridge's family relationships, must have been dazzling indeed. Sharing in the role of the "bad" and punitive father, Boyer
must have come close to outshining Frank in Coleridge's psychological drama. But let it be noted that he undertook the role of
the mother as well, performing with stunning accuracy in Coleridge's fantasy about a single, undifferentiated parent.

The explanation for this fantasy is to be found partly in the
circumstance that for a year after his father's death Coleridge
was alone, so to speak, with his mother. The bromide about the
widowed parent who finds it necessary to be both mother and father demonstrates in this instance the truth that generally underlies a worn-out phrase. In addition, and anterior to this first year
of mourning, the reversal of family roles that has been suggested
undoubtedly fed such a fantasy. But such a reversal, real or fancied, could have taken firm hold on his mind only if his oedipal
tensions were so disturbing that the reversal would have provided him with protection against his feelings about the "word
that is clothed about with Death—/ Mother of Love, & Fear, &
Holy Hope." It seems clear that the tensions were sufficiently
troublesome to require some such protection and that the reversal of sexual roles did help to provide it. Certainly the amiable
and passive Velez and the dangerous and punitive Alhadra in
Osorio represent an effort to effect such a reversal in his art.

Perceiving the mother in the role of aggressor who would
punish his fantasy of usurpation protects him in two ways. First,
it rids her of her most attractive quality—her femaleness—and
so enables him to deny his desire for her. Second, it makes her the
instrument of potential punishment, which is in his guilty consciousness more welcome than temptation, and provides him
with a censor. Similarly, perceiving the father in the role of pas-

sive and loving recipient of affection also protects him in two ways. First, it rids the father of his most valuable quality—his maleness—and so enables Coleridge to deny his wish to usurp him. Second, it successfully denies the capacity of the father to administer punishment.

iii

The phallic, or punitive, aspect of women is what Coleridge steadily and persistently saw, and it usually evoked from him, in self-defence, the response of the "child of frailty." Two boyhood poems, "Pain" and "Genevieve," show that the response was made early. In the poem "Genevieve" he wrote that

> I've seen your breast with pity heave,
> and *therefore* [sic] love I you, sweet Genevieve![38]

There is some evidence that "Genevieve" and "Pain" were written about the same time, while he was in the sick ward of Christ's Hospital, with his nurse's daughter in mind.[39] Together they make up a sketch for *Dejection*; the wish for pity in "Genevieve" combined with the contrast between health and sickness or then and now in "Pain" foreshadows the 1802 ode. "Pain" begins reminiscently, like the sixth stanza of *Dejection*:

> Once could the Morn's first beams, the healthful breeze,
> All Nature charm, and gay was every hour.[40]

It continues, and ends, with a far more explicit distinction between the poet and "the crowd" than is drawn in *Dejection* between the poet and the object of address; artistic elaboration here is even less complex than it is in *Osorio*:

> Ah what can all Life's gilded scenes avail?
> I view the crowd, whom Youth and Health inspire,
> Hear the loud laugh, and catch the sportive lay,
> Then sigh and think—I too could laugh and play
> And gaily sport it on the Muse's lyre,
> Ere Tyrant Pain had chas'd away delight,
> Ere the wild pulse throbb'd anguish thro' the night![41]

Crude self-pity and the aggressions it covers are all but refined
out of the *Dejection* ode; but although they are submerged they
are there nonetheless, and these two poems, which he said were
written "when the Author was a boy,"[42] make them very clear.

These same feelings—the aggressions underlying self-pity—
are expressed in Coleridge's letters to Mrs. Evans and her daughters, whom he met in 1788 in London as a result of his having
befriended young William Evans at school. Hanson writes that
Coleridge "leaped into intimacy with the family,"[43] a phrase that
describes very well his eagerness in beginning close relationships.
His first recorded letter to Mrs. Evans is dated February 13,
1792; its tone is familiar:

> ... my whole heart shall be laid open like any sheep's
> heart: my Virtues, if I have any, shall not be more
> exposed to your view than my Weaknesses. Indeed I
> am of opinion, that Foibles are the cement of Affection,
> and that, however we may *admire* a perfect character,
> we are seldom inclined to love or praise those, whom
> we cannot sometimes blame.[44]

Uncharacteristically, he comments on his good health, but not
without a reference to what he believed to be his "ugliness," as
if to ward off the evil eye that might punish such good luck:

> I am indeed at present most wonderfully well—and if
> I continue so, I may soon be mistaken for one of your
> *very* children: at least, in clearness of complexion,
> and rosiness of cheek I am no contemptible likeness
> of them, tho' that ugly arrangement of features, with
> which Nature has distinguished me, will, I fear, long
> stand in the way of such honorable assimilation.[45]

The mock-filial relationship has something flirtatious in it, to
which Mrs. Evans herself must have contributed if this letter is
any indication:

> But you are mistaken—I not only read *your* letter
> first, but, on my sincerity! I felt no inclination to do

otherwise: and I am confident, that if Mary had
happened to have stood by me, and had seen me take
up *her* letter in preference to her *Mother's*,—with
all that ease and energy, which she can so gracefully
exert upon proper occasions, she would have lifted up
her beautiful little leg, and kicked me round the room.
Had *Anne* indeed favor'd me with a few lines, I confess,
I should have seized hold of them before either of your
letters—but then this would have arisen from my
love of NOVELTY, and not from any deficiency in filial
respect.[46]

A later letter to Mrs. Evans is less playful, and reveals the
"child of frailty" once more, but with an outburst of anger that
recalls his fury toward the woman in Ottery who had suggested
that he should not escape whipping. The letter is dated February
5, 1793, four days before his letter to George in which he acknowledged Frank's death after an elaborate description of a decayed tooth, and begins with a description almost word for word
the same as the one he later wrote to George. It continues, after
this disarming preface, with a panegyric upon pity and a spitting
rage upon people who do not feel it:

... you are too frequently troubled with a strange
forgetfulness of yourself, and too too apt to go far
beyond your strength, if by any means you may alleviate
the Sufferings of others—[Mrs. Evans has been nursing
her sick brother; is this a subtle expression of jealousy?]
ah! how different from the majority of those, whom
we courteously dignify with the Name of human:—
a vile herd, who sit still in the severest distresses of
their *Friends*, and cry out, There is a Lion in the way!—
animals, who walk with leaden sandals in the paths
of Charity, yet to gratify their own inclinations will run
a mile in a breath. Oh! I do know a set of little, dirty,
pimping, petyfogging [sic], ambidextrous fellows, who
would set your house on fire, tho' it were but to roast

an egg for themselves! Yet surely—considering it
even in a selfish view, the pleasures that arise from
whispering peace to those who are in trouble, and
healing the broken in heart are far superior to all, the
unfeeling can enjoy.[47]

To Mary he writes two days later, using a metaphor that foreshadows the imagery of *Dejection*, that

I am so closely blocked up by an army of misfortunes,
that really there is no passage left open for Mirth or
anything else.[48]

In none of the letters to Mary is there anything stronger than
a mild flirtatiousness; it would be impossible, without the salutations, to distinguish the letters to Mary from the letters to her
mother.[49] All of his "passion" for her he expressed not to Mary
but to Southey, to whom he wrote afterward, apparently truth-
fully, "I never durst even in a whisper avow my passion, though
I knew she loved me,"[50] and Chambers is undoubtedly right
in saying that "he means 'could have dared' and 'even had I
known.' "[51]

Mild and insignificant as it was, this jolly play-acting at romance appears to have ended abruptly immediately after Coleridge heard of Frank's suicide. In 1793 there is only one letter to
the Evans family after the letter to George in which he discusses
Frank's death. This is a letter to Anne, already looked at in another context,[52] which begins by consoling her illness but soon
proceeds to bemoan his own feelings:

... within this last month I have lost a Brother and a
Friend! But I struggle for chearfulness.[53]

By the end of 1793, in the suicidal mood brought on by news
of Frank's death, he had long given up any notion of continuing
to see Mary, and in July of 1794 in a chance encounter at Wrex-
ham he went to some lengths to avoid being seen by her. He told
Southey that his reason for avoiding her was that he was too poor
to declare his love,[54] but the coincidence of his break with Mary

and the news of Frank's death is too strong to avoid the suggestion that he did not dare to continue to assert his masculinity,
even to this mild degree, in the face of such a powerful fulfillment of his wish to assert it. With the father symbolically dead
again, Mary—or any woman—becomes the *liebestod* heroine,
the "Mother of Love, & Fear, & Holy Hope," her phallic quality
frighteningly strengthened.

Coleridge expresses something like the fear of the phallic
woman in September of 1794, in a letter to Southey:

> ... my faculties & discernments are so completely
> jaundiced by vexation, that the Virgin Mary & Mary
> Flanders—alias Moll, would appear in the same hues.[55]

This juxtaposition of sanctity and sin, the promise of grace and
the threat of damnation, was possible for him in the month when
he became engaged to Sarah Fricker and was reminiscing about
his "passion" for Mary Evans. The value of the name *Mary*,
which he carefully splits between good and evil (surely his mod-
ification of *Moll* is an invention), is that it expresses neatly his
ambivalence toward Mary Evans.

A month later he received a letter from Mary which certainly
does not sound as though she had been the one to break off the
relationship:

> Is this handwriting altogether erased from your
> memory? To whom am I addressing myself? For
> whom am I now violating the rules of female delicacy?
> Is it for the same Coleridge, whom I once regarded as
> a sister her best-beloved Brother?[56]

But the purpose of the letter is to dissuade him from his plan
to form a Pantisocratic society in America and it seems possible
that Mary violated the rules of female delicacy at the suggestion
of George Coleridge[57] who was at the limits of his patience and
resourcefulness at this time.

Coleridge sent a copy of Mary's letter to Southey along with a
lengthy letter of his own which is devoted to a discussion of

Pantisocratic details and of his efforts to forget Mary. Sarah and
Pantisocracy he ranges on one side of him, and Mary on the
other, in a passage that has been quoted often enough:

> I loved her [Mary], Southey! almost to madness. Her
> image was never absent from me for three Years—
> for *more* than three Years.—My Resolution [to marry
> Sarah and become a Pantisocrat) has not faltered—
> but I want a comforter.—I have done nothing—I have
> gone into Company . . . I endeavored to be perpetually
> with Miss Brunton[58]—I even hoped, that her Exquisite
> Beauty and uncommon Accomplishments might have
> cured one Passion by another. The latter I could easily have
> dissipated in her absence—and so have restored my
> affections to her [Sarah], whom I do not love—but
> whom by every tie of Reason and Honor I ought to
> love. I am resolved—but wretched![59]

Three days later he wrote a short letter to Francis Wrang-
ham,[60] enclosing the sonnet, "Thou bleedest, my poor heart,"
which he had also sent to Southey. He says of the sonnet that

> It was occasioned by a letter (which I lately received
> from a young Lady, whom for five years I loved—
> almost to madness) dissuasive from my American
> scheme—; but where Justice leads, I will follow—
> though her Path be through thorns & roughness.[61]

Coleridge's habit of repeating his own words almost verbatim to
more than one correspondent is nowhere less persuasive than it
is here; and his characteristic transcendence of time does nothing
to strengthen his credibility.

There is quite simply no evidence that Coleridge ever loved
Mary Evans, let alone "to the point of madness" or thereabouts.
Certainly he never attempted to declare himself or to act upon
his "passion" until he had heard a rumor of her engagement to
another man.[62] With Mary safely unattainable he was able, in
November of 1794, to tell her openly that

For four years [apparently a safe middle ground between three and five] I have *endeavoured* to smother a very ardent attachment—in what degree I have succeeded, you must know better than I can. With quick perceptions of moral Beauty it was impossible for me not to admire in you your sensibility regulated by Judgment, your Gaiety proceeding from a cheerful Heart acting on the stores of a strong Understanding. At first I voluntarily invited the recollection of these qualities into my mind—I made them the perpetual Object of my Reveries—yet I entertained no one Sentiment beyond that of the immediate Pleasure annexed to the thinking of You. At length it became an Habit. I awoke from the Delusion, and found that I had unwittingly harboured a Passion which I felt neither the power or the courage to subdue. My associations were irrevocably formed, and your Image was blended with every idea. I thought of you incessantly: yet that Spirit (if Spirit there be that condescends to record the lonely Beatings of my heart) that Spirit knows, that I thought of you with the purity of a Brother. Happy were I, had it been with no more than a Brother's ardor![63]

As a declaration of love, this passage loses considerable force from its expression in terms of Hartleian psychology; it looks more like an exercise than an ecstasy. His awakening from his "Delusion" was no doubt brought about by the prospect of marriage with Sarah Fricker, and there is certainly more truth in his acknowledgment of brotherly "purity" than there is in his conventional bow to "more than a Brother's ardor."

By December 24 Mary had written to him to verify the news of her engagement, and he sent her a short note confessing that "In my wildest day-dream of Vanity I never supposed that you entertained for me any other than a common friendship."[64] Apparently he was able to sustain even this light flirtation only because Mary's attitude toward him never threatened him with the

possibility that the relationship might come to anything. The
note ends gracefully:

> To love you Habit has made unalterable. This passion
> however, divested, as it now is, of all Shadow of Hope,
> will lose it's disquieting power. Far distant from you
> I shall journey thro' the vale of Men in calmness.
> He cannot long be wretched, who dares be actively
> virtuous.[65]

Five days later he wrote to Southey, with his trick of unacknowledged quotation of himself:

> I am calm, dear Southey! as an Autumnal Day, when
> the Sky is covered with grey moveless Clouds. To *love*
> *her* Habit has made unalterable: I had placed her in
> the sanctuary of my Heart, nor can she be torn from
> thence but with the Strings that grapple it to Life.
> This passion however, divested as it now is of all
> Shadow of Hope, seems to lose it's disquieting Power.
> Far distant, and never more to behold or hear of her, I
> shall sojourn in the Vale of Men sad and in loneliness,
> yet not unhappy. He cannot be long wretched who
> dares be actively virtuous.[66]

But he goes on to contradict himself; if he expects absence to
dilute his feelings for her, it is not on the basis of his past experience, and in a rare burst of undisguised self-revelation which
settles and clarifies the nature of his "love" for Mary he reflects
that

> When she was present, she was to me only as a very
> dear Sister: it was in absence, that I felt those gnawings
> of Suspense, and that Dreaminess of Mind, which
> evidence an affection more restless, yet scarcely less
> pure, than the fraternal.[67]

In revery, alone, without the real woman, he fancied that he
loved her; but clearly her presence signalled to him a clear and
present danger. There is no doubt that he deliberately whipped

up the flow of feeling he expressed for Mary in the letters to
Southey, and that it served two purposes. It released some of his
latent erotic emotion for Southey, and it also gave him a reason,
however specious, for his reluctance to marry Sarah Fricker:

> To lose her!—I can rise above that selfish Pang. But to
> marry another—O Southey! bear with my weakness.
> Love makes all things pure and heavenly like itself:—
> but to marry a woman whom I do *not* love—to degrade
> her, whom I call my Wife, by making her the Instrument
> of low desire—and on the removal of a desultory
> Appetite, to be perhaps not displeased with her
> Absence![68]

Sexual intimacy is the result of "low desire" and it "degrades"
the woman unless it is accompanied by something he calls love.
But this perches him on a dilemma, since "love" apparently exists for him only if it is not sexual, only, in fact, in what he referred to as "revery" or "day-dream," without the dangerous presence of a real woman.

But on October 4, 1795, in fear and wretchedness, having as-
sured Southey that "I will do my Duty,"[69] he enacted his marriage
to Sarah Fricker and entered a period in which his need for punishment at the hands of an aggressive woman overcame that fear
and was willingly fulfilled by her, a period in which he was able
both to demand and to retaliate for such punishment by means
of the sexual relationship that he felt would debase her.

The quality of his feelings for Mary had resembled the quality
of his characterization of her namesake Maria in *Osorio*: it was
not "real." She was the image of the "good" mother, the image
of his own mother that was present to his conscious mind, who
evoked from him the response of the "child of frailty." Like the
Virgin Mary she was numinous and therefore tabu: "In [his]
wildest day-dream of Vanity [he] never supposed that [she] entertained for [him] any other than a common friendship," and
she was therefore an unequal adversary with whom he could not

possibly do battle, because like any goddess she would win and destroy him.

But Sarah Fricker was another matter; she was bound up in his mind with his "resolve," his "duty," to chasten his need for creature comforts by means of Pantisocratic renunciation of private possession. Within this aura she became a flesh-and-blood Alhadra with whom he could enter the lists without compunction, a "bad" mother, a Moll Flanders, the nursemaid Molly in thin disguise. With her the mask of the "child of frailty" could be allowed to crack, and the hostilities beneath could be a bit more safely released.

It seems clear that the only possible circumstances in which he felt free to behave sexually were those in which he could use such behavior to debase a woman and symbolically to punish his "bad" mother. Alhadra was an infidel and not worthy of total surrender to her destructive powers;[70] Sarah he did not "love," and she had no magical power in combat. The fear that Mary might utterly destroy him he recognized and partially expressed to Southey in December of 1794:

> Had I been united to her, the Excess of my Affection
> would have effeminated my Intellect.[71]

What this amounts to is fear of castration, a durable terror that is illustrated in *Christabel, Kubla Khan,* and the *Rime.*

4. Sleep and Poetry: *Christabel*

I must devote some one or more Days exclusively to the Meditation on Dreams. *Days? Say rather Weeks!*—
Coleridge

i

Basically, *Osorio* and all Coleridge's major poems tell the same story: the story of paradise lost. The earliest evidence for his sense of a fall from grace is to be found in the account of his runaway experience; and the most comprehensive enlightenment on the nature of his feelings at the time of that experience and later is to be found in a fairly long dream he recorded in his notebook. The major poetry is the result of attempts to repeat what was apparently his most painful and impressive childhood experience, his running away from home. In the repetition of this experience, he was trying, as everyone with a repetition compulsion tries to do, to understand it and to transcend it. His poetry, like his letters, is part of his lifelong effort to define himself, to understand himself, and to gain control over the conflicting parts of his nature. But the long dream recorded in his notebook provides an explanation for the failure of the poetry to make the effort successfully.

The relationship of the dream to the poetry is complicated. All the major poems had been completed—as nearly as they were ever to be—before the dream. The dream-work, as a result, contains images and associations that refer both to his primary experience and to what perhaps I may call his secondary experience: his poetry. The dynamic relationships of his conscious life,

his unconscious life, and his poetry were apparently so painful to
him that he said he could not finish *Christabel* or *Kubla Khan*,
and for almost twenty years he could not bring these poems fully
to light.[1] Judging from the preponderance of material from his
secondary experience in his dream, I should say that the process
of writing verse existed for him between conscious and unconscious levels of knowing, in more than one way: first, the poetry
mitigated between the conscious and unconscious experience
much in the same way that the ego mitigates (or litigates) between the superego and the id; and second, the act of writing
proceeded from unconscious drives and at the same time re-excited these drives and threatened to bring them into consciousness. The result, since the unconscious drives were tabu, was
pain; and when the pain became severe enough, the writing had
to stop.

The pains of Coleridge's sleep, therefore, will go a long way
toward explication of his poetry, of his difficulty in finishing it,
and of the cessation of serious poetry after 1802. The dream I
want to look at is recorded on October 3, 1802, the day before
Wordsworth's marriage to Mary Hutchinson and the publication
of the *Dejection* ode, seven years after Coleridge's marriage to
Sarah Fricker and three years after hé met Sara Hutchinson who,
according to too many writers, was the object of his frustrated
love.[2]

October was a big month in Coleridge's life.[3] He was born on
October 21, 1772. His runaway experience occurred in October,
1780. His father died on October 4, 1781. He married Sarah
Fricker on October 4, 1795. Mary Evans married Fryer Todd on
October 13, 1795. He met Sara Hutchinson on October 26,
1799. And on October 4, 1802, Wordsworth married the sister
of the woman Coleridge believed he loved, and the poem *Dejection* saw its first publication. It is a matter of some interest, therefore, that he recorded an account of a dream in his notebook on
the night of October 3, 1802, a night in which the most signifi-

cant events of his life apparently converged in their influence
on his emotions, through their association with the month of
October, and heightened in intensity on the eve of a day that
must have been in prospect loaded with emotional power. It is
worth remarking that Coleridge, the great inquirer into the
mazes of the mind, recorded it for the ostensible purpose of demonstrating the nonexistence of the element of surprise in dreams:

> October 3—Night—My dreams uncommonly illustra-
> tive of the non-existence of Surprize in sleep—I dreamt
> that I was asleep in the Cloyster[4] at Christs Hospital
> & [had] awoken with a pain in my hand from some
> corrosion/ boys & nurses' daughters peeping at me/
> On their implying that I was not in the School, I
> answered yes I am/ I am only twenty—I then recollected
> that I was thirty, & of course could not be in the School
> —& was perplexed—but not the least surprise that
> I could fall into such an error/ So I dreamt of Dorothy,
> William and Mary—& that Dorothy was altered in
> every feature, a fat, thick-limbed & rather red-haired—
> in short, no resemblance to her at all—and I said, if I
> did not *know* you to be Dorothy, I never should *suppose*
> it/ Why, says she—I have not a feature the same/
> & yet I was not surprized—
>   I was followed up & down by a frightful pale woman,
> who, I thought, wanted to kiss me, & had the property
> of giving a shameful Disease by breathing in the face/
>   & again I dreamt that a figure of a woman of a gigantic
> Height, dim & indefinite & smokelike [?snakelike][5]
> appeared—& that I was forced to run up to it—& then
> it changed to a stool—& then appeared again in another
> place—& again I went up in great fright—& it changed
> to some other common thing—yet I felt no surprize.[6]

The dream begins in Christ's Hospital, where he was sent to
school shortly after the death of his father. This first detail expresses a telescoped past, made up of more than one stage of

experience, that is common enough in dreams. The general anxiety of the dream appears to refer to his unconscious memories of his father's death and of his being sent away to school, in close juxtaposition, in a causal relationship, as if being sent away to school had seemed to him a punitive exile. Such a relationship is supported by subsequent details: he is lying in bed,[7] having awakened "with a pain in [his] hand from some corrosion." *Corrosion* is an odd word here; it suggests something more than injury or soreness—the connotation is of decay, as if his hand, the instrument of his will, were being eaten away as punishment for what he had willed it to do (go at Frank with a knife? murder his father?). The corrosion of the hand, in this context, becomes a clear symbol of the fear of castration brought about by the usurping fantasies that accompany autoeroticism.

Children are "peeping" at him in a projection of the latent exhibitionism (whose other face is latent voyeurism) that is noticeable in his letters. The presence of more than one sex in the peepers indicates confusion about his own sexual nature and also about the sexual nature of others who had looked at him in the past. In his account of his runaway episode, he wrote that he was finally brought home in the early morning and that he remembered, "and shall never forget, my father's face as he looked upon me while I lay in the servant's arms . . . My mother . . . was outrageous with joy."

Another suggestion in the detail of the peeping children is called up when these children imply that he is not "in the School," a memory of feeling excluded, unloved, alienated. These are the feelings that led him to run off in rage and fear[8] when he was a child at Ottery and that surely were not exorcised but were probably aggravated by guilt through his having punished his parents for the punishment he thought they had inflicted on him.

The reference to and confusion about his age has significance in this context as well as in another; it suggests that he is indeed relating the past and the present, as he says "yes I am/I am only twenty—I then recalled that I was thirty, & of course could not be in the School;" and it also indicates the presence in his mind of his approaching birthday—he is to be thirty in eighteen days —a reminder that he is growing older and closer to death. The sense of alienation that attended—justifiably or not—his early childhood in the family apparently attended also his later child-hood in the school where "How, in my dreams, would my na-tive town (far in the west) come back, with its church, and trees, and faces! How I would wake weeping, and in the anguish of my heart exclaim upon sweet Calne in Wiltshire!"[9] Perhaps in the dream, as he has awakened, it is from just such a dream as one of these he recalls.[10]

Into the dream at this point, where the sense of fear and alien-ation is strong, slip the figures of Dorothy, William, and Mary— the three people to whom Coleridge repeatedly turned as to a three-personed family,[11] for comfort and refuge from his un-happy marriage, his ill health, and his painful attraction to Sara Hutchinson. His behavior toward them was frequently that of an unhappy and demanding child, and there is no doubt that in the closest period of their friendship he caused Wordsworth and more particularly Dorothy the kind of anguish that only a highly sensitive and extremely verbal child can cause its parents.[12] Dor-othy in the dream does not appear to be Dorothy at all; and the description of her appearance is unattractive. Sara Hutchinson is noticeably absent, a fact that might suggest the strongest hos-tility toward her, the wish to deny her existence, if it were not that Sara's actual physical appearance, as it is detailed by Cole-ridge's daughter, seems to be attached to Dorothy in the dream:

> She had fine, long, light brown hair [Dorothy is given
> red hair, of course], I think her only beauty, except
> a fair skin, for her features were plain and contracted,
> her figure dumpy, and devoid of grace and dignity. She
> was a plump woman, of little more than five feet.[13]

Dorothy then, who does not seem to be Dorothy in the dream, is a Sara substitute upon whom it was less painful to displace feelings of revulsion, though these feelings are even in the dream strongly denied by doubt of her identity.

Behind the Dorothy/Sara figure in the dream is the shadow of the phallic mother, who emerges almost immediately afterward, separated from it by the dream-logical transitional image of

> a frightful pale woman[14] who, I thought, wanted to
> kiss me, & had the property of giving a shameful
> Disease by breathing in the face/[15]

—a perfectly transparent expression of a *gestalt* of feeling that surrounds the incest fantasy: physical desire (projected on to the woman who "wanted" to kiss him) accompanied by shame, revulsion, and fear. The fear of corrosion or castration earlier in the dream reaches a crescendo here; it becomes openly a fear of death, as evidenced by the word *disease* capitalized. It is the *liebestod* situation that is being enacted, but with its usually submerged elements brought to the surface; and the agent of punishment shifts from its weak character as father—William Wordsworth (flanked, it should be noticed, by two women, as if they were guarding him and also as if they "belonged" to him rather than to the dreamer)—to its far more powerful character as phallic mother, just as it was seen to shift in *Osorio*.[16]

As in a glissando the "woman of a gigantic Height" begins to coil about his mind. The "gigantic Height" demonstrates another effort of the dreamer's censor to disguise Sara, who was "of little more than five feet;" it also indicates with perfect clarity the "word that is clothed about with Death—/ Mother of Love, & Fear, & Holy Hope,"[17] the mother who is both loved and feared, and who would seem, in the small boy's past that is present to this dream, to be truly gigantic.

The phallic nature of the mother is indicated not only by the "gigantic Height" of the figure but also, and more openly, by the metamorphosis of the woman into a "stool." The word *stool* may have meant to Coleridge a (low) seat or a (high) throne.[18] Since the woman subsequently changes "to some other common thing," however, the chances are that the idea of a throne was not in his mind, unless with unconscious irony. A ready association to *stool* as seat would have been *close-stool*[19] for the man who all his life was inordinately interested in his digestion; and from this association it is only a quarter-step to the woman as something to be literally got rid of.

The image of the woman as something to be literally got rid of makes sense of the dream in a number of ways. For one thing, it coincides with the woman's serpentine appearance, disappearance, and double metamorphosis, eluding him each time he is "forced to run up to it," winding in and out of the dream in response to his wishes and terrors. It coincides also with the earlier revulsion toward women in the dream; and at the same time it counteracts the revulsion, the fear, by reducing the woman to the level of contempt. Another effect of the image is to suggest a submerged content in Coleridge's salute to Sara Hutchinson in the first draft of the *Dejection* ode: "A Heart within my Heart!"[20]— content which I am afraid must destroy the rainbow of his alleged love for her for good. Or perhaps for ill. The woman he would have liked to love was really within him ("her" character is ambiguous like all dream imagery; her appearance as *stool* is, as noted above, phallic); his "love" was pure narcissism; and at some level of consciousness he was struggling to get rid of the passive female element in his personality, or at least to deny that the "heart" within his "heart" was there literally.

ii

This dream of 1802 goes back not only to Coleridge's early and late childhood but also to the poetry he had written not long before. The dream begins as he has awakened from sleep—a detail that indicates that the dream-work is relatively close to consciousness, or at least that it exists between deep sleep and wakefulness; from this it is clear that the material of the dream is to be related more strongly to the present and the recent past than it is to the remote or primeval past. It is not surprising, then, that this material should echo elements of Coleridge's poetry.

The "frightful pale woman," for instance, who "had the property of giving a shameful Disease by breathing in the face," is a dangerous woman like Alhadra in *Osorio* and the longing for and fear of punishment by death, which in *Osorio* is expressed by making Alhadra the executioner, binds the two female figures even more closely. In fact it ought to be said that for Coleridge, as for Blake and Lawrence and Eliot, all women are one woman; it is only their disparate aspects, as projections of his ambivalence, that people the drama of his verse: the women are either "good" mothers or "bad" mothers or involuntary confusions of the two, and their "goodness" or "badness" is always intensified beyond any concern with the representation of reality.[21]

The parallel between the dream and *Christabel* is clear in a general way, since Geraldine is obviously a "bad" mother: she struggles with Christabel's "good" mother for the possession of the heroine's soul, she seduces Christabel (as the dream-woman "wanted to kiss me"), she appears to corrupt (corrode?) Christabel, she is certainly as loathly a damsel as the "frightful pale woman," she is described in serpentine imagery, and in a simile that appears to be an involuntary confusion of "good" and "bad" (or conscious and unconscious) under the guise of literary irony she is openly compared to a mother:

> And Lo! the worker of these harms,
> That holds the maiden in her arms,
> Seems to slumber still and mild,
> As a mother with her child.[22]

But there are also less obvious resemblances between the dream and the poem. Structurally, for instance, the dream-work proceeds very much in the manner of the poem. Both begin at night: the poem opens upon midnight, the time of sleep; and the dream begins as the dreamer wakes from sleep. Christabel's alienation is then established, just as the dreamer's sense of alienation is established: she is not like others, since she is awake when everyone else is asleep; she is praying for her lover who is far away; and she has only one parent—her mother is dead. So with the dreamer: in the dream he is waking as others watch; we know that he believes his "love" to be far away;[23] and we know that he has only one parent—his father is dead. And in both the dream and the poem a dangerous woman attempts seduction. Although the seduction is successful in the poem and not in the dream, the results of seduction appear in both—corruption enters Christabel as she is possessed by Geraldine, and the dreamer fears corrosion or castration and death. That decay ends the poem—or the so-called fragment of it—but begins the dream implies that the sleep from which the dreamer believes he has awakened carried material that had to be repressed: successful seduction can be taken as a prior situation of the dream.

The general anxiety of the dream—the causal juxtaposition of memories of his father's death and of his being sent away to school—is operative in the poem but it is elaborated in so many ways that it is almost successfully concealed. The elaboration begins to fail, however, toward the end of Part II, when Christabel falls at her father's feet:

'By my mother's soul do I entreat
That thou this woman send away!'
She said: and more she could not say:
For what she knew she could not tell,
O'er-mastered by the mighty spell.[24]

The spell appears to correspond to Coleridge's repression of his fantasies of usurpation; the jealousy which Sir Leoline imputes to Christabel[25] has its counterpart in Coleridge's unconscious rivalry with his brothers and his father; and the plea for punitive exile of Geraldine corroborates the conclusion that Coleridge

unconsciously equated his being sent away to school with punishment.

These correspondences point to the chief method of elaboration in the poem: sexual reversal. In a poem where metamorphosis and confusion between appearance and reality are dominant, it is not surprising that the chief metamorphosis, the most
significant confusion, is applied—consciously or not—to the major persona. Christabel is in effect the heart within Coleridge's
heart, the female element in his personality; and the triangular
situation involving her with her father and Geraldine is a transparent expression of the triangular situation involving Coleridge
with his mother and father.

If Geraldine is the "bad" or phallic mother and Christabel is
a mask[26] for Coleridge, these two female figures are also, paradoxically, both projections of Coleridge—a paradox which the
dream gives proof, since Geraldine is powerfully related to the
"frightful pale woman" by the feelings of desire and disgust
which both evoke, since she is a figure which enters, by means of
the notion of demonic possession, into Christabel's nature, and
since her serpentine nature corresponds to the dream disguise of
the "stool." What appears to be emerging in the poem is that the
heart within the heart can be related to Geraldine the "bad" or
phallic mother as a symbol of Coleridge's identification with his
mother, the result of his incorporation of the female rather than
the male parent. The element of demonic possession in the poem
is a beautiful sublimation of incorporation. This distorts to some
degree the conventional family triangle; and it suggests that the
primeval rivalry in Coleridge was directed not only toward his
father but toward his mother as well. Such an interpretation of
his tensions accounts for the complicated elaboration in the poem
and also for the insatiable emotional demands he made in his life
on everyone who was close to him. The fact seems to be that he
wanted to "be" both his mother and his father: the fantasies of
usurpation represent the desire to "be" the father; the fantasies of

passivity—the conceit of the child of frailty, the nympholeptic quest, and the emotionally ambiguous letters to his male friends —represent the desire to "be" the mother, in a sexual alliance with the father. This explanation should not be taken as flat statement or as simplification: the passive fantasies serve more than one purpose. Besides their demonstration of female identification through incorporation, their value as a disguise for fantasies of usurpation should not be overlooked.

The presence in Coleridge of these two powerful wish-fantasies means simply that it was impossible for him to behave in a fully masculine way; and it explains the force of his narcissism, since it seems clear that whenever Coleridge thought he was in love, he was actually attempting two things at once: the purgation of the female within him and the reconciliation of his male and female needs. The tension between these two opposite attempts caused the failure of both.

iii

Such tension is fully demonstrated in the doubling device that dominates *Christabel* much in the same way that it dominates dreams. In the dream already looked at, the phallic mother is multiplied not doubled; and the multiplication produces various disguises for her: the peeping children, Mary, Dorothy, Sara, the frightful pale woman, the woman of gigantic height, and the stool. The logic of the poem, since it is apparently an effort to explore his own guilts, and to control the self, is dream logic not dramatic logic. The female doubling of Christabel and Geraldine is complicated. They are first of all two aspects of childhood: they are both daughters. In addition they are redoubled in their mothers. Christabel's mother is of course dead; Geraldine's mother is conspicuously absent (as Sara is conspicuously absent in the dream), but there are links between Geraldine and the baron's mastiff bitch:

> Sir Leoline, the Baron rich,
> Hath a toothless mastiff bitch;
> From her kennel beneath the rock
> She maketh answer to the clock,
> Four for the quarters, and twelve for the hour;
> Ever and aye, by shine and shower,
> Sixteen short howls, not over loud;
> Some say, she sees my lady's shroud.[27]

The hound is not simply a detail borrowed out of Gothic romance; it is the first image in the poem that overtly expresses the supernatural: there is a strong possibility that the hound communicates with the land of the dead, the underworld, hell—all metaphors for the unconscious—where western poets have traditionally located the deep truth; "Some say, she sees my lady's shroud." Given the absence of capital letters, "my lady" must refer to Christabel's dead mother, and the passage links the hound with Geraldine in three ways. First, they are both female. Second, Geraldine also has access to the underworld and communicates with the dead mother:

> But soon with altered voice, said she—
> 'Off, wandering mother! Peak and pine!
> I have power to bid thee flee.'
> Alas, what ails poor Geraldine?
> Why stares she with unsettled eye?
> Can she the bodiless dead espy?
> And why with hollow voice cries she,
> 'Off, woman, off! this hour is mine—
> Though thou her guardian spirit be,
> Off, woman, off! 'tis given to me."[28]

Third, the hound and Geraldine both "belong" to the baron; the hound literally belongs to him, and Geraldine "belongs" to him in the same way that Dorothy and Sara Hutchinson "belong" to Wordsworth in Coleridge's dream, which is to say that Geraldine, like those two women, is an obstacle to exclusive love with the male figure and at the same time is the object of love herself, unattainable because she "belongs" to someone else.

The parallels between Geraldine and the mastiff bitch—except for the detail of "belonging," which is probably produced unconsciously—appear to be deliberate; in a poem where every persona has a double, the double for Christabel's dead mother might be the mastiff bitch, who would then be taken as the mother of Geraldine.[29] The hound communicates with Christabel's dead mother but also with Geraldine. When the two women walk toward the baron's castle, the hound is disturbed:

> Outside her kennel, the mastiff old
> Lay fast asleep, in moonshine cold.
> The mastiff old did not awake,
> Yet she an angry moan did make!
> And what can ail the mastiff bitch?
> Never till now she uttered yell
> Beneath the eye of Christabel.
> Perhaps it is the owlet's scritch:
> For what can ail the mastiff bitch?[30]

What ails the mastiff bitch is not only that an evil spirit is about to enter the sanctified territory (Christabel's home) which she is guarding, as a watchdog, but also that she perceives—in sleep—the presence of a dangerous figure (Geraldine) which she herself, as mother, has produced. This perception of Geraldine, in sleep, is a microcosm of Coleridge's own dream experience; the "angry moan" is a signal of danger; the danger is just such a danger as the one that Coleridge produced in his dream of October 3, 1802. If the mastiff bitch is a watchdog, it corresponds precisely to the censor that persists not only in Coleridge's waking life but also in his dreams. On the level of dramatic verisimilitude, the "angry moan" is strictly appropriate: what other response could be expected from the mother of an evil spirit?[31]

All the female personae in the poem are manipulated as elaborations of the female aspect of Coleridge's personality; and the doubling of Christabel and Geraldine is redoubled in their mothers as further elaboration of Coleridge's incorporation of his mother. Counting up the number of female figures in the poem, we find five: two living (Christabel and Geraldine), one dead (Christabel's mother), and one that appears to be missing but is actually disguised (Geraldine's mother).

This female round-up has a precise counterpart among the male figures, who are similarly doubled and redoubled. On the purely dramatic level, Sir Leoline has his double in Lord Roland de Vaux of Tryermaine; they are both fathers. But their relationship is as distorted as the relationship between the mothers of Geraldine and Christabel; Roland's existence is never verified in the poem, just as Geraldine's mother's existence is disguised. Considering the name *Roland* along with certain details in Gillman's account of Coleridge's plan for the conclusion of the poem,[32] it appears that Roland is related not only to the living father and to Geraldine's disguised "bad" mother, but also to the dead "good" mother: like his namesake the legendary Roland, and like Christabel's dead mother, he is powerless to contribute to the situation—he is impotent, a neatly imagined contrapuntal correspondence to the female element in Coleridge, the heart within the heart.

Just as the female personae represent aspects of Coleridge resulting from the incorporation of his mother, so the male personae represent aspects of Coleridge's personality resulting from the attempt to incorporate the father. One of these is Bracy the bard, the "good" father: he has poetic insight and his dream is a prophetic vision whose emblems reveal the deep truth; knowing that Christabel is a dove endangered by a serpent, he is more understanding and more protective of her than the baron is; from this it follows, first, that he is the result of Coleridge's repression, which stimulated protestations of affection for his dead father, and, second, that like Christabel he represents an idealized image of Coleridge to himself—a narcissistic projection.[33]

Counting up the male figures in the poem, we find that their number equals exactly the number of female figures. There are again five: two living (Sir Leoline and Bracy), one dead or at least non-existent (Lord Roland), and one that appears to be missing (Christabel's absent lover). Since the apparently missing female figure turns out to be the mastiff bitch, it is logical that the absent lover of Christabel may also appear in the poem in disguise.

The likeliest figure for the disguise of the lover is to be found, like a hidden picture in a puzzle design, in Geraldine's account of her abduction:

> Five warriors seized me yestermorn,
> Me, even me, a maid forlorn:
> They choked my cries with force and fright,
> And tied me on a palfrey white.
> The palfrey was as fleet as wind,
> And they rode furiously behind.
> They spurred amain, their steeds were white:
> And once we crossed the shade of night.
> As sure as Heaven shall rescue me,
> I have no thought what men they be;
> Nor do I know how long it is
> (For I have lain entranced I wis)
> Since one, the tallest of the five,
> Took me from the palfrey's back,
> A weary woman, scarce alive.
> Some muttered words his comrades spoke:
> He placed me underneath this oak.[34]

It cannot be an accident that Geraldine's kidnappers are five in number, corresponding to the five male figures in the poem.[35] Of course she is not to be trusted; the whole of her account may be a lie (another example of her resemblance to Coleridge, whose reliability where facts were concerned was practically non-existent); she is after all an evil spirit. But we are dealing not with dramatic logic here but with dream logic; and within such a context, Geraldine's story seems "true" for the poem.

The five kidnappers, in their redoubling of the five chief male personae, provide powerful emphasis for virility; they appear to be the collective, archetypal male, behaving with full masculine aggression (the hint of sexual assault is *only* a hint; but what other motivation could there be for this group project?) which carries, inevitably for Coleridge, the association of death, this time in the form of the pale horses and of Geraldine's description of herself as "scarce alive." The paradox that the kidnappers make a victim of the evil Geraldine is resolved in the reflection that in this poem the dramatic personae are in reality projections of Coleridge's own states of mind: Geraldine as an aspect of Coleridge is "right" in her combination of victimizer and victim. The conclusion to be drawn here is that for Coleridge, perhaps consciously, the victim is actually in collusion with his victimizers, inviting and even enjoying attack. Christabel, it will be remembered, *invites* Geraldine to sleep with her;[36] and there is no doubt that the result for her is what Coleridge referred to in "The Pains of Sleep" as "desire with loathing strangely mixt."[37]

What the poem seems to say is that this is the way men behave when they are not distracted or inhibited by the guilt that creates sentimental love: they kidnap, with force and fright, they brutalize, they abandon their women after they have "once . . . crossed the shade of night." Since it appears to be necessary for Christabel to pray for "the weal of her lover that's far away,"[38] it seems likely that he is on a journey involving some danger not only to his person but also—and more important—to his virtue. "The tallest of the five" who kidnap Geraldine is the disguise for Christabel's absent lover, the demon-lover who is always hiding behind Coleridge's sentimental mask;[39] and it is significant that he puts her down beneath the oak where Christabel finds her.

iv

These are the labyrinthine ways Coleridge took in *Christabel* to explore his guilts under the pretext of exploring the nature of evil;[40] but unlike Theseus he had no Ariadne to thread him out again, and the labyrinth turns out to be a dead end, an impasse. The poem remains unfinished because to Coleridge the nature of his guilts had to be repressed. The frenetic attempts, in *Christabel*, to define evil as "vice" (the homoerotic relationship as expressed in the encounter of Geraldine and Christabel) or as blind authority (Sir Leoline's failure to understand Christabel and his simultaneous failure to recognize the evil in Geraldine) represent in the one case the attempt to locate evil within himself and in the other case the attempt to locate it outside himself. He was closer to reality in the effort to find evil in himself, and he seems to have been aware of this, judging from his attempt in the conclusion to Part II to relate Sir Leoline's feelings to his own; but since he persisted in feeling his fantasies as vice, the images of truth which his poetry-making called up from his unconscious terrified him.

Terror in the presence of his own ambivalent feelings of love and animosity—toward men as well as toward women—had led him as a child to read his prayer-book in an effort to convince himself that he was a "good" child while "thinking *at the same time* with inward and gloomy satisfaction, how miserable my Mother must be!" and it led him in *Christabel* to reproduce precisely the same duality:

> The lovely lady, Christabel,
> Whom her father loves so well,
> What makes her in the wood so late,
> A furlong from the castle gate?
> She had dreams all yesternight
> Of her own betrothed knight;
> And she in the midnight wood will pray
> For the weal of her lover that's far away.[41]

The repetition compulsion appears to lie beneath this stanza, forcing the elaboration of the runaway episode, complete with fantasies ("dreams . . . /Of her own betrothed knight") and prayer. The reading of *Christabel* deepens our awareness of the significance of that childhood experience, since although Christabel is praying for her lover (male), she is entirely open to Geraldine's advances; and although she suffers from them, there can be no doubt about her pleasure in the midst of pain:

> With open eyes (ah woe is me!)
> Asleep, and dreaming fearfully,
> Fearfully dreaming, yet, I wis,
> Dreaming that alone, which is—
> O sorrow and shame! Can this be she,
> The lady, who knelt at the old oak tree?[42]

The word *yet* in the middle of the third line quoted above has considerable force in this context; taken together with the hiatus in the description of the dream, it can only point to Christabel's collusion and pleasure in what Coleridge thought of as vice.

There is actually more reluctance in Geraldine than in Christabel in the face of intimacy:

> They crossed the moat, and Christabel
> Took the key that fitted well;
> A little door she opened straight,
> All in the middle of the gate;
> The gate that was ironed within and without,
> Where an army in battle array had marched out.
> The lady sank, belike through pain,
> And Christabel with might and main
> Lifted her up, a weary weight,
> Over the threshold of the gate:
> Then the lady rose again,
> And moved, as she were not in pain.[43]

This is one of Christabel's active moves; the second is giving Geraldine the elixir, to strengthen and make her "most beautiful."

In this passage, Christabel takes the key and opens a door in an iron gate—"ironed within and without"—; Lowes and Nethercot, perhaps out of reticence, both missed this evidence of a clear though perhaps unconscious association in Coleridge's mind to Marvell's "To His Coy Mistress," where "the iron gates of life" are unmistakably a metaphor for the procreative organs, male and female. Eroticized fear and hostility motivate this passage, as is borne out not only by the detail of "the gate that was ironed within and without" but also by the reference to "an army in battle array" which had marched out of this gate; what some writers[44] have called sadism in Coleridge and in other Romantic poets appears here: it is the result of what has been emphasized repeatedly in this chapter as ambivalent feelings of love and hostility complicated in Coleridge's case by the direction of these feelings toward both sexes. The fantasies that accompanied his running away when he was a child were very likely as complicated and as much in tension with each other as the elaborations in *Christabel*. They would have had to be an early expression of his two opposite attempts: to purge the female within him and to reconcile his female and male needs.

That these tensions are not vice is obvious; but in the presence of infantile feelings of love and animosity for his father, or for a man who represented his father, clearly Coleridge was overcome by the sorrow and shame that runs its recurrent way through *Christabel*. The infantile nature of the homoeroticism in the poem is indicated by the emphasis on fathers and mothers and by the duplication of daughters; in addition, in the passage describing the physical intimacy between Geraldine and Christabel, not only is Geraldine compared to a mother, but also Christabel is compared twice to a child—once in the simile already looked at: "As a mother with her child," and again in the stanza that describes what looks like relaxation after a sexual encounter:

And see! the lady Christabel
Gathers herself from out her trance;

Her limbs relax, her countenance
Grows sad and soft; the smooth thin lids
Close o'er the eyes; and tears she sheds—
Large tears that leave the lashes bright!
And oft the while she seems to smile
As infants at a sudden light![45]

The childlike nature of Christabel makes it necessary to look
more closely at the story of paradise lost in the poem. This story
cannot be too strongly emphasized, since it recurs throughout
Coleridge's poetry, major and minor, as early as "Pain," whose
approximate date is 1790, and as late as *Dejection.* Obviously he
did feel he had lost something. His four major poems—two of
them allegedly unfinished—show more clearly than the others
the progression from then to now, from paradise to exile, from
innocence to corruption, from action to paralysis.

In order to determine what this progression meant to him and
what it was exactly that he felt he had lost, the original of the
progression ought to be reconsidered. Both in *Genesis* and in
Milton's poem there are three personae and a piece of scenery—
the tree of the knowledge of good and evil. The three personae
correspond to a primeval triangle, two males and a female; and
the action, in which the satan/serpent figure charms Eve away
from Adam, is a double metaphor. First, it is a metaphor of the
male fantasy of usurpation: the satan/serpent figure is Adam's
usurping aspect, with the result that, as Adam "loses" Eve, what
he has really lost is his virility; he is metaphorically castrated as
punishment for his fantasies of usurpation (projected by the cre-
ators of the myth onto the satan/serpent figure, as though Adam
were not responsible for them). The punishment is extended further to death, as the most important result of the fall is mortality.
Second, this episode is a metaphor of the male fantasy of hostility
toward the female, again conveniently projected outside the self
onto the satan/serpent figure; the result, the punishment, is lust
rather than love—which again alienates him from Eve, makes

him "lose" her in a sense—together with mortality. The function
of the tree of the knowledge of good and evil in this double fantasy is to represent, by means of its value as a symbol of male divinity, knowledge that is tabu, as the knowledge of the mother's
sexuality is tabu to the son; and that it is Eve who is persuaded by
the satan/serpent figure to eat of its fruits is another projection,
similar to Coleridge's dream of the woman who "wanted" to kiss
him. The fruit of the forbidden tree corresponds both to the son's
attraction toward his mother and to his witnessing the primal
scene—love between the parents, both of which produce knowledge that is tabu.

In *Christabel*, as in *Genesis* and in Milton's poem, the ostensible loss is innocence; the progression is from innocence to corruption. And in the light of the dream that has been analyzed, it
can be seen that corruption to Coleridge meant corrosion or castration or death. Given this equivalence, the loss expressed in the
poem must be the loss of something that is opposite to corrosion
or castration or death—so that what is lost in *Christabel*, as well
as in his other major poems, is health or virility or life.[46]

The poem opens in an Eden, Christabel's sheltered home. But
Christabel, like Eve, has wandered away from the shelter and has
stopped beneath a tree. There are signs of the possibility of regeneration, but they are weak: the cock crows earlier than usual,
but only drowsily; "the night is chilly but not dark." These signs
can also be taken as evidence that a dream-world is in control, so
that regeneration is possible through the kind of deep truth that
is to be found in dreams; but the possibility is not very strong.
"The thin gray cloud" that "covers but not hides the sky" is like
sleep—or repression—that covers but does not destroy reality;
reality, or the deep truth, is there, in the shape of the moon, but
although the moon is full it is, like Christabel's eyes after sleeping with Geraldine, "both small and dull."[47]

Christabel, like Eve, is tempted beneath the tree (the mistletoe
on this tree is another evidence of Christabel's ambiguous sexual

nature),[48] and like Eve she is open to temptation and succumbs.
There follows, in Part II, the inevitable exile, her alienation from
her father, prepared for throughout the poem by the deliberate
creation of a world of night and death.

v

It is significant that the alienation is complete only after Christabel has seen her father and Geraldine embracing:

> And now the tears were on his face,
> And fondly in his arms he took
> Fair Geraldine, who met the embrace,
> Prolonging it with joyous look.[49]

There is some reason for assuming that this embrace is an elaboration of the primal scene, since seeing it produces in Christabel
both fear and the memory of having seen Geraldine undressed
the night before, together with tactile recall of the embrace that
Christabel had enjoyed with Geraldine. The whole sequence of
details following the embrace of the Baron and Geraldine suggests the persona's imaginative identification with at least one
partner—her father—in the performance, accompanied by a
powerful sense of tabu:

> Which when she viewed, a vision fell
> Upon the soul of Christabel,
> The vision of fear, the touch and pain!
> She shrunk and shuddered, and saw again—
> (Ah, woe is me! Was it for thee,
> Thou gentle maid! such sights to see?)[50]

But confusion arises here, since it is clear that Christabel identifies not only with her father as she watches the embrace but also
with Geraldine. After the scene stirs her memory of the events
of the night before, she becomes *like* Geraldine; the sight makes
her hiss like a snake, as she demonstrates the result of possession
(Coleridge has produced an unconscious pun in his description of
possession) by the snakelike Geraldine:

Again she saw that bosom old,
Again she felt that bosom cold,
And drew in her breath with a hissing sound.
Whereat the Knight turned wildly round,
And nothing saw, but his own sweet maid
With eyes upraised, as one that prayed.[51]

It should be noted that when her father turns "wildly round" at the sound of the hissing, he sees nothing but his "sweet" daughter in an attitude of prayer. Like Coleridge as a child, Christabel adopts the mask of prayer to disguise both knowledge that is tabu and the unacceptable emotions that such knowledge produces. Again Christabel is "praying" in an effort to prove herself a "good" child, just as she prayed beneath the tree, and just as Coleridge prayed while enjoying thoughts of how miserable he was making his mother. Furthermore, in seeing and in being seen, Christabel reflects not only Coleridge's latent voyeurism but his latent exhibitionism as well. The narrative details suggest rather strongly that the source and nature of Coleridge's guilt was the actual or fantasied witnessing of the primal scene.

Christabel's encounter with Geraldine appears to be her descent into hell; and the intention of the poem is probably to suggest a Blakean progression in which this descent will reveal the deep truth about the self so that regeneration can take place in the form of enlightened virtue. But the ambiguity that surrounds the two female figures is such that it prevents any regeneration through self-recognition. Geraldine and Christabel both have equivocal natures: it is never clear that one or the other is either fully "good" or fully "bad," fully the aggressor or fully passive, fully victimizer or fully victim; and underlying all of this is the fact that their sexual identities are as vague as any element in the poem.

Christabel's active/passive role has already been pointed out; and the most vivid illustration of sexual ambiguity in Geraldine's nature is the horrified description of her undressing:

> Her silken robe, and inner vest,
> Dropt to her feet, and full in view,
> Behold! her bosom and half her side—
> A sight to dream of, not to tell!
> O shield her! shield sweet Christabel![52]

Exactly how horrified this description is can be gauged by the difficulty Coleridge had in writing it. In one variant version, after the dash in the third line above, there is the detailed observation that "her bosom and half her side/ Are lean and old and foul of hue."[53] Many suggestions radiate from this line. First, the fear of incest is apparent in the age that is revealed; second, the breast is clearly corroded, an indication that Geraldine is a female *manqué* if not a phallic woman; since corrosion apparently meant castration to Coleridge, it is entirely possible to see Geraldine also as a castrated or feminized male. The final suggestion, which is the culmination of all of these, is that Geraldine fully represents the single, undifferentiated parent apprehended in infancy.

The force of the incest fear comes through in the succeeding stanza, where Geraldine has great difficulty in lying down with Christabel:

> Yet Geraldine nor speaks nor stirs;
> Ah! what a stricken look was hers!
> Deep from within she seems half-way
> To lift some weight with sick assay,
> And eyes the maid and seeks delay;
> Then suddenly, as one defied,
> Collects herself in scorn and pride,
> And lay down by the Maiden's side!—[54]

Coleridge had equal difficulty in writing this passage. He revised the line that immediately precedes it five times:

> And she is to sleep with Christabel.
> And she is to sleep by Christabel.
> And must she sleep by Christabel.

And she is alone with Christabel.
And must she sleep with Christabel.[55]

When he got to this passage, it began originally:

She took two paces and a stride,
And lay down by the maiden's side,[56]

and there is evidence of strain and indecision in another manuscript (italicized words in brackets were struck out):

She gaz'd upon the maid, [*she sighed*]
[*She took two paces and a stride,*]
Then
[*And lay down by the Maiden's side.*][57]

It is only when Geraldine "collects herself in scorn and pride" that she is able to take Christabel in her arms, just as Coleridge was able to enter marriage only with a woman who evoked the same feelings in him. *Christabel* appears to be one of Coleridge's attempts to control the disorganized aspects of the self; the reason the poem is so full of confusion is that his attempts to sort out, let alone to control, the warring parts of his personality were unsuccessful. The multiplication of the phallic mother in his dream has its parallel in *Christabel*, where the interrelationships of the identities of the personae seem to be the result of such multiplication of himself, undertaken unconsciously, so that attempts at self-recognition had to fail because they were accompanied by precisely the kind of self-deception that is present in the record of his dream as well as in his letters.

vi

Coleridge was extremely proud of his metrical achievement in *Christabel*; and despite the fact that it is exactly like the "tumbling verse" of the sixteenth century, he was at pains to point out its novelty.[58] This kind of insistence could be based in his lack of confidence in the value of the poem, which some writers have referred to.[59] But the effect is to call attention to the form; and such attention reveals that not only is the form relevant to the overt material but in addition it is relevant to the submerged material that has so far been discussed. One of the chief characteristics of the ballad form is of course repetition, which would have made it extremely attractive to Coleridge as a vehicle for his unconscious repetition compulsion. Furthermore, the ballad was thought of in Coleridge's time as an extremely old form, so that it was eminently suitable for the expression of his primeval feelings. And finally, the famous meter, to which at least one writer[60] has attributed subliminal effectiveness, achieves that effectiveness by means of rocking, syncopated rhythms that suggest not so much sexuality as autoeroticism, a form of behavior that is always accompanied by fantasies like those that *Christabel* appears to elaborate.

The question remains whether or not *Christabel* is an unfinished poem. As a literary work it appears to be both finished and unfinished. The narrative of course is incomplete: Bracy's quest as well as Geraldine's father and Christabel's lover are suspended elements that can be accounted for only by means of the poem's submerged structure and not on a purely dramatic level. But the two parts of the poem are of nearly equal length; and as a form of the paradise lost story it is as complete as Milton's poem, which also ends with alienation. The difference is that the possibility of regeneration, or grace, in *Christabel* is far weaker than it is in Milton's Christian story. It has been suggested that *Christabel* is incomplete because of Coleridge's inability to accede to the value of the Christian story.[61] The suggestion is probably valid, as far as it goes; but underlying and producing Coleridge's cosmic pessimism was his profound pessimism concerning his ability to behave in a fully masculine way.

It seems likely that the poem is incomplete, as a literary work, mainly because of what has already been proposed: that writing it re-excited his unacceptable unconscious drives to the point of extreme discomfort, so that Coleridge could not continue his elaboration. But it appears to me that psychologically the poem is finished. As a vehicle for expressing tensions that he could express in no other way, *Christabel* did its work completely and effectively. When Coleridge had finished with the release—temporary, to be sure—of these tensions, when he had fully expressed his fantasies, he had also finished with the poem.

5. Sleep and Poetry:
The Rime and *Kubla Khan*

Some painful Feeling, bodily or of the mind/ some
form or feeling has recalled a past misery to the Feeling,
& not to the conscious memory—I brood over what
has befallen of evil.—Coleridge

i

The *Rime of the Ancient Mariner* is of course finished, as a literary work, even though its conclusion was bought at the price
of some lines that look as though they had been embroidered on
a sampler. It was Coleridge's second sustained attempt, after *Osorio* and before *Christabel*, at self-recognition and self-control under the pretext of an exploration of the nature of evil and within
the narrative framework of the paradise lost story. The reason it
is finished, as *Christabel* is not, and the reason it is artistically
superior to *Osorio*, is that in it Coleridge found a form of elaboration that was more effective than the forms he used in *Osorio*
and *Christabel*: a narrative device for expressing brilliantly the
essentially unfinished business he undertook repeatedly in his
poems. The ancient and durable notion of the man condemned
to live forever and to relate forever the circumstances of his experience is perfectly suited to the repetition compulsion that
forced Coleridge to write again and again different versions of
the tension between the fantasies of usurpation and the fantasies
of passivity. It may very well be this tension that is responsible
for the ambiguities in the *Rime* that have produced such a pro-

84

liferation of interpretations in our time[1] and that produced in
Coleridge's time the innocent nonsense of the Barbauld exchange.[2]

The recurrent motifs of *Osorio* and *Christabel*, and of his runaway experience and the dream of October, 1802, appear to be
operative in the *Rime*. For one thing, uncertainty about his own
sexual nature may account for the image of the dead bird that
hangs around the mariner's neck, as though it were an emblem
of displaced genitalia, which suggests the female both in the
analogy to the breast and in its force as attribute of the primitive
mother goddess, but which also suggests the male (passive, to be
sure) in its pendent position. The bird is dead, as Geraldine's
bosom was corroded; so that not only sexual ambiguity but also
sexual mutilation is again in evidence. The encumbrance is the
result of the murder, which is itself an ambiguous act; in the
light of the dualistic values that seem to arise from the dead bird,
it may perhaps be assumed that the murder represents not simply
the fantasy of usurpation of the father (punished by castration)
but in addition the fantasy of passivity or identification with
the mother and also the fantasy of aggression toward the "bad"
mother. It is a serious mistake to label the "crime" of the poem
in a one-to-one equivalence, as simple allegory: both Coleridge's
theory of symbol and his complicated and simultaneous drives in
various directions preclude such an easy solution.[3]

Further evidence of sexual confusion can perhaps be found
in the serpentine, or phallic, imagery about which the mariner
feels first one way and then another. The blessing "unaware" of
the water snakes reveals not only a regenerating regard for "the
one life"[4] but also unconscious homoeroticism which, since it
follows punishment in the poem, corresponds in function to the
unconscious homoeroticism in Coleridge's personality as a defense against aggressions toward the father. Having first expressed animosity toward the snakes, the mariner eventually
finds it expedient to deny the animosity by means of his uncon-

scious blessing. So with Coleridge; the fantasy of usurpation is generally followed by the retreat to the pose of the "child of frailty."

The progression from innocence to corruption/castration, from Eden to exile, is expressed as plainly as it is in *Christabel*; the "grace" the mariner achieves is not very strong, since his punishment of exile from the human race in the form of eternal life[5] and eternal confession powerfully outweighs it. Latent exhibitionism is expressed in the detail of the men who curse him with their eyes (compare the children "peeping" at him in the dream as well as the need to be judged that appears to motivate his "confessional" letters), and latent voyeurism makes his eyes glitter like Geraldine's.

The dream image of the "frightful pale woman who, I thought, wanted to kiss me, & had the property of giving a shameful Disease by breathing in the face" is anticipated by the Nightmare Life-in-Death and in fact by the whole complex of ship, woman, and man, in which again the strongest agent of punishment by far is female—the ship is, conventionally enough, referred to as "she," and the Nightmare is the dominant figure in the pair that stand on deck; furthermore, in the dice game it is the female who "winneth the ancient Mariner:"

> And is that Woman all her crew?
> Is that a DEATH? and are there two?
> Is DEATH that woman's mate?
> *Her* lips were red, *her* looks were free,
> Her locks were yellow as gold:
> Her skin was white as leprosy,
> The Nightmare LIFE-IN-DEATH was she,
> Who thicks man's blood with cold.[6]

Here is not only the "cold" of Geraldine's bosom, but also the lips that "wanted to kiss me," the "frightful" pallor, and the disease which, although it is not shameful, certainly evokes extreme terror and revulsion; and these follow a stanza that suggests, in the image of the pair on deck, the primal scene, in which the woman's "mate" is indeed death in three ways: first, he is the father who is both dangerous (capable of retaliatory punishment) and in danger (vulnerable to usurpation); second, he is the father literally dead, perhaps as a result of usurpation and perhaps at the hands of the mother in a sexual encounter (she does after all win the dice game); third, he is the threat of death that attaches to the phallic mother, who is capable of destroying not only the father but the son as well.

It is only after the mariner has watched the woman and her mate dicing for his destiny that the nature of his punishment is made clear to him—not death, but life-in-death: an interesting correspondence to the alienation, or exile, that punishes Christabel after she has witnessed the equivalent of the primal scene. Two conclusions can be drawn from this sequence of events: first, that the dice game parallels Coleridge's childhood experience when he felt that "My Father was very fond of me, and I was my mother's darling," which is to say that he felt that his parents were in competition (perhaps sexual) for him (a projection of his conflict between two sets of loyalties and affections); second, that witnessing the primal scene—actually or in fantasy—was the source of his tension between usurpation and passivity and that it was also the chief source of all his guilts, the source and nature of evil for which he looked so laboriously and so long.

ii

King Oedipus tore out his own eyeballs after he discovered that he had literally acted out his father's role with his mother; Athene blinded Teiresias after he had seen her in her bath;[7] primitive people equate the eye both with power and with genitalia (and things equal to the same thing are equal to each other); psychiatric patients make similar equations and punish themselves for unacceptable visual knowledge—because such knowledge is accompanied by fantasies of participation in the scene

being enacted—by developing somatic symptoms of eye disease.[8]
In a dream recorded in Coleridge's notebook, dated Friday night,
November 28, 1800, a date when Dorothy Wordsworth wrote
in her journal that Coleridge had "walked over" to Grasmere,
that he was "very unwell," and that "He went to bed before
Wm.'s return. Great boils upon his neck,"[9] we find these details:

> —a most frightful [note that this word is repeated in
> the dream of 1802, and in a similar context] Dream of
> a Woman whose features were blended with darkness
> [like Dorothy in the dream of 1802, who had "not
> a feature the same"] catching hold of my right eye &
> attempting to pull it out—I caught hold of her arm fast
> —a horrid feel [revulsion again]—Wordsworth cried
> aloud to me hearing my scream—heard his cry &
> thought it cruel he did not come/ but did not wake
> till his cry was repeated a third time—the Woman's
> name Ebon Ebon Thalud—When [the word *my*
> deleted] I awoke, my right eyelid swelled—[10]

This dream appears to have existed even closer to consciousness than the dream of 1802, judging from the circumstance that
Coleridge actually heard Wordsworth calling to him and ad-
justed the sound to the dream, and from the fact that Coleridge
screamed aloud during the dream. It is safe to assume then that
the dream was stimulated by present events and that being at
Grasmere in the company of William and Dorothy Wordsworth
was "like" being at home with his parents, so that it reinforced
the anxieties that produced both the boils and the dream. This
cozy *ménage à trois* (which, by the way, had already shown signs
of disorganization[11]), far from being the sheltered and suppor-
tive situation that many writers take it to be[12] in an effort to explain the so-called *annus mirabilis*, was saturated with dangers
for Coleridge; and his courting of it closely resembles his efforts
to attach himself to another man and to tie the knots so tightly
that they broke.

The dream expresses animosity toward both the mother and the father; but characteristically, the mother is by far the stronger figure since she is the direct agent of punishment by castration (eye equals genitalia; also, eye equals instrument for forbidden knowledge) while the father figure is "cruel" only in that he does not come to the dreamer's rescue: he is, like Roland in *Christabel*, and like Coleridge's own father, powerless to contribute to the situation, partly because this phallic mother would already have castrated him (in the case of Wordsworth and of Coleridge's own father before he died) and also because she might have been responsible for his death.

It seems fairly clear that it is Wordsworth who represents the father in the dream. Evidence that it is Dorothy who represents the mother, besides the fact that the dream can be seen as a response to present events, is a little subtler. In the first place, this dream woman's features resemble the features of Dorothy in the later dream: in both cases, the features are ambiguous. In the second place, the last part of the woman's name is an intricate anagram of the sounds of Dorothy's name, with the substitution of one liquid consonant (l) for another (r). The name as a whole, Ebon Ebon Thalud, translates as Black Black Dorothy, or dangerous, or evil, or revolting, Dorothy, which should probably be taken as a variant of the dangerous phallic mother Alhadra in *Osorio*, who is of course also black. The "Woman whose features were blended with darkness" then is not only a detail that points indirectly to Dorothy in the matter of ambiguous features (and therefore of disguised features that signal the mother behind the mask); it is also one that points directly to Dorothy as the "bad" mother.

The "bad" mother in this dream appears to be punishing Coleridge for having unacceptable visual knowledge, in exactly the same way that Athene punished Teiresias, and in a projection of Coleridge's own wish for punishment that was exactly like the wish of King Oedipus, who fulfilled it himself. This dream provides powerful support for the conclusion that the nature and source of all Coleridge's guilts can be directly traced to his having witnessed or imagined the primal scene.[13]

The correspondence of the "Woman whose features were blended with darkness" to the "frightful pale woman who, I thought, wanted to kiss me, & had the property of giving a shameful Disease by breathing in the face," to the Nightmare Life-in-Death whose "skin was white as leprosy," and to the black-complexioned Alhadra, is not vitiated by the apparent contrast between pallor and blackness.[14] What is responsible for the contrast is the unconscious censor in Coleridge's personality that attempted to disguise the object of his desire, anger, and fear. Contrast is a fairly weak form of disguise, which indicates that the unconscious material he was trying to repress in his dreams and to elaborate in literature must have been threateningly close to consciousness. This is underscored by the nature of both the dreams that have been looked at: both of them existed close to consciousness; and it seems to be borne out, furthermore, by the difficulties Coleridge had in writing *Christabel* and by the uncomplicated form of elaboration in *Osorio*.

The unconscious material is of course more successfully controlled in the *Rime* than it is in the dream of 1800. The mariner does not go blind like Teiresias or Oedipus; but he is afflicted by an eye disorder that enables him to compel or to fascinate his listener so that he "cannot choose but hear," even though he hears in extreme discomfort. On the narrative level, the mariner is endowed with the compensatory "sight" that was given to Teiresias —and also to Oedipus—in exchange for physical blindness; the mariner has seen the deep truth in a form of underworld or hell, and although he is punished for it, he can use his forbidden visual knowledge to make others suffer by telling them about it. Psychologically, as he fixes his listener with his glittering eye, he is attempting to draw him into his own fantasy; and if the eye/genitalia equivalence is recollected, it can be seen that this fantasy includes veiled homoeroticism: his listener is a male. In this single detail of the fascinating eye Coleridge managed to subsume all his efforts to inflict pain on others and to establish quasi-homoerotic relationships.

The mariner, then, is a type of visionary, up from hell. Like Adam he has tasted forbidden fruit and he is punished by exile. In its main outlines, however, the *Rime* corresponds not only to the paradise lost story but also to the runaway experience about which Coleridge wrote to Poole. Like Coleridge as a child and like Christabel (and also like Eve: the mariner is not fully male), the mariner wanders from safety (the shore), he commits a violent act (chronology is reversed with relation to the runaway experience; and yet psychologically it is not reversed: the violent act can be committed only in an alien world, the kind of world De Quincey postulated for Macbeth's murder of the king), and he makes expiation. The last detail parallels Christabel's prayers under the tree and her praying pose before her father and also Coleridge's childhood prayers on the banks of the River Otter; and it is by means of this parallel that the question of the "moral" in the *Rime* is resolved. Mrs. Barbauld was psychologically right, although for the wrong reasons. The motto which concludes the *Rime* seems false in exactly the same way that the self-deluding prayers of the angry little boy were false.

iii

The rivalrous feelings that made Coleridge angry as a child appear to provide the dominant theme in *Kubla Khan*, although the circumstances of its publication and some of the critical positions that have been adopted with regard to those circumstances have tended to obscure this situation.[15] Various writers have recently argued the case for *Kubla Khan* as a complete work[16]—and no one needs to argue for its musical and visual brilliance—but no one so far has suggested that a psychological reading of the poem adds another dimension in support of their efforts: one

way in which it achieves its completeness is by means of the rhe-
torical opposites of "he can" and "I cannot."

Without going into the argument that *Kubla Khan* is a poem
about poetry,[17] it is possible to see that it is indeed a poem about
action, of whatever kind, including poetic. The first thirty-six
lines describe Kubla Khan's action, a *fait accompli*, and the rest
of the poem describes the persona's incapacity for action, with
the important proviso that if he could act, he could improve on
Kubla Khan's accomplishment.

The nature of the action is, literally, constructive: Kubla Khan
has constructed the pleasure-dome and the garden around it; the
persona cannot construct a similar dome, although if he were to
find what he has lost he could do so. Furthermore, the Khan has
merely "decreed" his construction but the persona would build it
himself and with nothing more material than music.

It is almost as difficult to determine the value of what Kubla
Khan has decreed as it is to distinguish between Geraldine and
Christabel. It may be helpful to consider that the artifact from
which everything else in the first thirty-six lines proceeds is the
pleasure-dome, with its submerged suggestion not only of
breasts[18] but of the *mons veneris* as well. The Khan therefore
presumably found the heart within the heart, the woman whose
presence can be detected behind at least the first eleven lines.

> In Xanadu did Kubla Khan
> A stately pleasure-dome decree:
> Where Alph, the sacred river, ran
> Through caverns measureless to man
> Down to a sunless sea.
> So twice five miles of fertile ground
> With walls and towers were girdled round:
> And there were gardens bright with sinuous rills,
> Where blossomed many an incense-bearing tree;
> And here were forests ancient as the hills,
> Enfolding sunny spots of greenery.[19]

Here is Adam with his Eve in Eden, complete with tree. Having "decreed" Eve, in the form of the pleasure-dome, he is obeyed not only in her creation[20] but also by means of the construction of boundaries—walls and towers—that delimit this paradise whose fertility is not merely agricultural. The pleasure-dome is built near the river; furthermore, the river is "sacred," its name suggests a primeval force through association with the first letter of the Greek alphabet, and it runs "through caverns measureless to man." Both the juxtaposition of the dome with the river and the attributes of the river itself strongly suggest a sexual substructure of associations here. It looks as though the Khan is powerful, as though "he can," because he is capable of full sexual expression. That the force represented by the river is sexual (an interpretation not in conflict with the reading of the river as "life"[21] but rather in extension of it) is further demonstrated by the primeval aura that floods the stanza: the lush fertility of the place must depend at least in part on age since "here were forests ancient as the hills." The walls that delimit the garden correspond to the gate in *Christabel* that was "ironed within and without;" but these walls have their companion pieces in towers, so that they are not formidable in this stanza but are in harmony with the full masculine assertion that the towers suggest.[22] The "caverns measureless to man" relate to the walls as female imagery, and the river relates to the towers as an image of male assertion; in this stanza they appear to be working together, as though the caverns were measureless in that they provide infinite space for the river to run through, infinite scope for the free assertion of the male.

But in addition to its other Edenic characteristics, the description in stanza one is strongly marked by recurrent sibilant sounds, like an echo, *sotto voce*, of the serpentine hissing in *Christabel*, so that the reader is beautifully and subtly prepared for line twelve, where fear sets in and casts an ironic color on the imagery of sexual harmony that has been set up in the first stanza. The dramatic situation has changed from its character as objective reportage to something like awe-struck editorial. The shift is emphasized by the conjunction *but* which signals an alternative point of view toward the situation in stanza one.

> But oh! that deep romantic chasm which slanted
> Down the green hill athwart a cedarn cover!
> A savage place! as holy and enchanted
> As e'er beneath a waning moon was haunted
> By woman wailing for her demon-lover!
> And from this chasm, with ceaseless turmoil seething,
> As if the earth in fast thick pants were breathing,
> A mighty fountain momently was forced:
> Amid whose swift half-intermitted burst
> Huge fragments vaulted like rebounding hail,
> Or chaffy grain beneath the thresher's flail:
> And 'mid these dancing rocks at once and ever
> It flung up momently the sacred river.
> Five miles meandering with a mazy motion
> Through wood and dale the sacred river ran,
> Then reached the caverns measureless to man,
> And sank in tumult to a lifeless ocean:
> And 'mid this tumult Kubla heard from far
> Ancestral voices prophesying war!
> The shadow of the dome of pleasure
> Floated midway on the waves;
> Where was heard the mingled measure
> From the fountain and the caves.
> It was a miracle of rare device,
> A sunny pleasure-dome with caves of ice![23]

The fear that emanates from this passage produces again, as in *Christabel*, the "desire with loathing strangely mixt" of "The Pains of Sleep." The adjective *sacred* of the first stanza gives way here to *savage* and *enchanted*, separated by *holy*—all words which recall the "Word that is clothed about with Death—Mother of Love, & Fear, & Holy Hope." The demon-lover makes his non-appearance as he does in *Christabel* ("woman" is only "wailing" for him), and he does so just before the source of the sacred river is revealed as a "mighty fountain" in a context that suggests both a caricature of ejaculation and the explosive physical details Coleridge drew in his letters. Read as a fantasy of male sexual behavior, this passage provides plenty of justification for the overt fear that is expressed when "'mid this tumult Kubla heard from far/ Ancestral voices prophesying war!" Most important is the assumption that what woman really wants as a lover is a demon-lover, an assumption that is made in order to justify the unconscious impulse to behave cruelly if not murderously toward woman. The demon-lover is the precise counterpart of the five abductors of Geraldine; apparently this is the only way Coleridge could look at male sexuality—as behavior that was cruel and destructive. In support of reading the demon-lover as the fully developed male, there is the detail of the fountain that is the source of the sacred river, producing not only holy water but also "huge fragments" and "dancing rocks," so that sexuality is seen to be achieved only as a by-product of violent aggression.[24] The result is punishment by death, as the sacred river, having "reached the caverns measureless to man," sinks "in tumult to a lifeless ocean"—an image of annihilation far stronger than the river's end in stanza one, which was only "down to a sunless sea." There is no doubt at this point that the river is annihilated by the female, since its end—in both stanzas—is brought about within "the caverns measureless to man." Again, the fear of the phallic woman as executioner shivers through this poem as it shivers through *Osorio*, *Christabel*, and the *Rime*, in correspondence to the unconscious fantasies that are uncovered in Coleridge's dreams; and the conflicting attitudes toward sexuality— "desire with loathing [and fear] strangely mixt"—are once more expressed.[25]

Another dimension explains even more fully the force of the "ancestral voices prophesying war." For Coleridge, sexuality was

not only violence toward women but also usurpation of the father's place. Kubla Khan is in this context a double metaphor: he
represents both father and son. It is to be assumed that his po-
tency includes the power to usurp, a form of male leadership that
is demonstrated repeatedly in the Greek myths where prophecies
of disaster are most frequently to be found; the adjective *ancestral* refers to the paternal vengeance that threatens him, complicated in Coleridge's fantasies, as the vengeance is attributed not
only to the father but to the mother as well and even more
strongly. The rhetoric of rivalry established in the poem, however, points not only to Kubla's value as a son who has successfully usurped his father, but also to his value as a father who is
vulnerable, in his turn, to usurpation at the hands of a son; it is
on this second level that the full meaning of the "war" that is
prophesied in the poem becomes clear: it is the durable war between the generations, created by the chain of contagion that
makes the child the father of the man.

The stanza ends in profound ambivalence. The "stately pleasure-dome" has become only its "shadow;" and it exists "midway"
between fountain and caves, and psychologically midway between fertilizing sun and life-killing ice. The ambivalence that
ends this stanza produces the image of the "Abyssinian maid,"
who is black, that introduces the final stanza of the poem, an
image that has precisely the same force as the dream image of
the "frightful pale woman who, I thought, wanted to kiss me, &
had the property of giving a shameful Disease by breathing in
the face," in another instance of disguise by means of contrast.

In an effort to reinforce the disguise, and to deny that the
"Abyssinian maid" was beyond the pale (in the same way that
Geraldine, the nightmare Life-in-Death, and Alhadra, a Moor,
were cut off from the world of normal possibilities), he wove this
image into another variety of the heart within his heart:

> A damsel with a dulcimer
> In a vision once I saw:

It was an Abyssinian maid,
And on her dulcimer she played,
Singing of Mount Abora.
Could I revive within me
Her symphony and song,
To such a deep delight 'twould win me,
That with music loud and long,
I would built that dome in air,
That sunny dome! those caves of ice!
And all who heard should see them there,
And all should cry, Beware! Beware!
His flashing eyes, his floating hair!
Weave a circle round him thrice,
And close your eyes with holy dread,
For he on honey-dew hath fed,
And drunk the milk of Paradise.[26]

Coleridge appears to say here that the reason the Khan "can" and he "cannot" is that he has purged the female element in his personality: he cannot "revive within [him] her symphony and song." One conclusion to be drawn from this declaration is that Coleridge's own sexuality was fed by more than one spring, that it depended on the passive, female aspect of his personality. That he felt he could not revive within him this essentially female sexuality, since it is at odds with his wish to purge himself of it, seems to be the result of the repression of his passive, female fantasies. Because these fantasies appear to be threatening consciousness in *Kubla Khan*, the need for an extra effort at repression is evident.[27] The tension in the poem is the tension between the surge of unacceptable emotions and the force of repression; and it is this tension that produces the ambiguities in the poem that make it continuingly provocative of exegesis.

iv

The connection between Coleridge's female sexuality and his unconscious desire for (and fear of) the phallic woman is that he wanted a woman who was like a man (or a man who was like a woman); and the archetypal object of his paradoxical desire was of course his mother.

It is the mother who seems to be at stake in the rivalry that is established in the poem between Kubla Khan and the narrator, between the man "who can" and the man "who cannot." What the narrator wishes is that, like the Khan, he could "decree" his Eve and his Eden of sexuality; what he mourns is, like all Edens and Golden Ages, something he has never had. It becomes apparent that the Khan's dominant characteristic is his paternity and that the description of the Eden in stanza one is another description of the primal scene. Stanza two continues the description, with overtones of horror that result from the son's identification not only with the father but also with the mother ("woman wailing for her demon-lover"); it is as if stanza one reported the primal scene and stanza two imagined that scene from the point of view of the narrator, as if he were enacting it in a double role, like the double role revealed in *Christabel*. Profound sexual ambiguity results from such identification; the male river, for example, actually springs from the fountain that is within the female "deep romantic chasm."[28]

Stanza three, then, is Coleridge's defense against his imaginative enactment of both parents' roles; it is his elaboration of the fantasy of performing with two partners in the primal scene. As a defense, it is still another literary parallel to his prayers on the banks of the River Otter when he was a child. In the poem, as on that occasion, he attempts to make himself numinous in order to deny his aggressions; the narrator becomes a poet-priest, a visionary (like the mariner) of whom it has traditionally been noted that he is dangerous: "And all should cry, Beware! Beware!" But the dangers in this visionary are that what he sees is tabu and what he imagines is violence both against the mother, since her phallic quality makes her a powerful opponent, and against the father, in the form of murderous usurpation. The explicit cause of danger in the narrator is that "he hath . . . drunk the milk of Paradise," a declaration that should remove any doubt about the maternal nature of this forbidden paradise or about the infantile nature of Coleridge's rivalry with his father. What he wanted was mother's milk.

The motifs that have appeared so far in Coleridge's primary and secondary experience as well as in his dreams are clearly discernible in *Kubla Khan*. Uncertainty about his sexual nature is expressed in the detail of the Abyssinian maid, in the rhetoric of "he can" and "I cannot," in the female origin of the male river, and in the duality of identification in the second stanza. The fantasy of usurpation punished by castration appears in the transition from the second stanza, where usurpation is imagined in fear, to the third stanza, where usurpation is denied by means of a variation of the conceit of the "child of frailty," and by means of the poem's larger progression from a view of Eden to a sense of exile. Voyeurism, the witnessing of the primal scene, is in strong evidence; and exhibitionism is expressed in the poem's last seven lines, beginning with the line, "And all who heard should see them [the dome and the ice, which, incidentally, recall the cold of Geraldine's bosom] there." The phallic mother, who appears elsewhere more overtly as a dangerous woman, is elaborated in the form of the Abyssinian maid and underlies the whole rhetoric of rivalry in the poem, from beginning to end. The device of multiplication is also brought into the poem, in the ambiguous character of the Khan; although he is predominantly the father, the imaginative enactment of his role blurs the distinction between the Khan and the narrator, and between the Khan and his "creation," the female, so that, in the second stanza particularly, the two emerge as aspects of Coleridge's personality, expressing both the fantasy of usurpation and the fantasy of passivity. And the correspondence of the Abyssinian maid to the Khan's pleasure dome indicates that again the mother has been split, or multiplied, or doubled, into the "good" mother of stanza one, where the dome functions harmoniously with the river, as in the proper role of wife, and the "bad" mother of stanza three, where the possibility of the persona's performance with the mother evokes danger. The "woman wailing for her demon-lover" represents still another variety of phallic or "bad" mother.

Whenever a literary work results in confusion, there are bound to be some readers who declare that what is apparent confusion is in reality the attempt of the writer to reconcile opposites;[29] if they do not invoke Blake's observation that "without contraries is no progression," they are at least to be commended for that, since the strength of Blake's aphorism is precisely that it does not imply the Hegelian thesis-antithesis-synthesis, but rather the ability to sustain opposites in dynamic interrelationship. Flatly, there is absolutely no reconciliation of opposites in *Kubla Khan*. There are opposites, but rather than being reconciled they remain in extreme tension. The confusion in the poem appears to be the result of Coleridge's inability to exist with any degree of comfort in a psychological marriage of heaven and hell.

It is no wonder that Coleridge failed to release *Kubla Khan* publicly for almost twenty years and that when he did release it, he felt compelled to attach one of his characteristic apologies to it;[30] the preface, like the whole of the elaboration in the second and third stanzas, functions precisely as his childhood prayers functioned when he ran away from home: it is another effort to show himself as a "good" man, a child of frailty.

There can be no doubt that *Kubla Khan* is not the result of an opium dream. It is a "dream poem"[31] in exactly the same way that *Osorio, Christabel,* and the *Rime* are "dream poems," which is to say that like his other verse, *Kubla Khan* is a product of what Coleridge referred to as the secondary imagination which, he said, was "co-existent with the conscious will,"[32] but that it owes perhaps even more to what he called fancy than he was willing to acknowledge.

6. Knowing and Being: Research and Experience

Metaphysics make all one's thoughts equally corrosive on the Body by the habit of making momently & common thought the subjects of uncommon interest & intellectual energy.—Coleridge

From the point of view of aesthetics, Coleridge's theory of the imagination has been looked at through microscope and telescope;[1] and his reliance on earlier (as well as contemporary) writers is now so well demonstrated that the ground of originality on which the theory was once assumed to rest has been largely cut from under it.[2] What remains to be shown is the psychological substructure of both the theory and the unacknowledged critical dependency.

It should be easy to see that the dependency on other writers is another example of the functioning of the passive, female aspect of Coleridge's personality, and that his failure to acknowledge this dependency represents an attempt to deny it. But it is a signal characteristic of these writers who fed him ideas that their thinking was anything but passive. Every one of them has his place in the shift, beginning in the Renaissance (for the western world at least), from *a priori* reasoning to inductive logic, from a god-oriented to a man-oriented point of view, from the medieval notion of original sin to the Kantian ontological crisis which seemed to make it possible for every man to create himself. They are all products of the conflict of science and faith and contributors to the increasing secularization of thought that was going on in Coleridge's time; their attempt was largely participation in, if not usurpation of, divinity.

The convulsions of the science-religion conflict are shown in Ernst Cassirer's *Philosophy of the Enlightenment*,[3] where he traces in some detail the content of what, it is clear,[4] was Coleridge's intellectual milieu. The effort to live peacefully on equal terms with God is plainly and repeatedly demonstrated by Cassirer as he discusses the development of thinking away from a static conception of the personality toward a dynamic one. The setbacks of the Reformation, with its reemphasis on original sin, were only temporary; man was committed to self-assertion and nothing could stop him. Writing of Leibniz, Cassirer says:

> To ... doctrines ... of metaphysical "transcendence"
> as well as the empirical form of "immanence," Leibniz
> opposes his own viewpoint. He upholds the postulate
> of immanence, for everything in the monad is to be
> derived from itself. But in that he intensifies this
> principle, he not only finds it impossible to return to
> God, but equally difficult to return to nature in the usual
> sense of the word. A difference between the nature of
> mind and the nature of things and a one-sided dependence
> of the former on the latter can no longer be maintained.[5]

The dynamic nature of personality has thus been established and the condition of assertiveness is discovered in man. It extends to religion:

> Henceforth religion is not to be a matter of mere
> receptivity; it is to originate from, and to be chiefly
> characterized by, activity.[6]

And it extends to psychology and epistemology. I cite here a phrase of Tetens's because it is oddly anticipatory of Coleridge.[7] Reacting against the sensational way of knowing, in an effort to show that the poetic faculty is not merely synthetic but is primarily creative, he used the phrase "plastic power of the imagination." Coleridge, engaged in similar efforts, "coined" the word "esemplastic" as an epithet for the imagination.[8]

Such efforts to define the poetic power as active not passive, as a condition of assertiveness that would be "like" the power of God to create the universe, are traceable in origin not directly to the German idealists or to the *philosophes*, but to Shaftesbury, as Cassirer reminds us in his summary:

> Rational analysis and psychological introspection, according to Shaftesbury, leave us on the periphery of the beautiful, not at its center. This center is not to be found in the process of enjoyment, but in that of forming and creating . . . For the difference between man and God disappears when we consider man not simply with respect to his original immanent forming powers, not as something created, but as a creator . . . Here man's real Promethean nature comes to light; he becomes "a second maker, a just Prometheus under Jove."[9]

Of course these are efforts toward participation in divinity and not toward its usurpation; man the creator is a "just" Prometheus, and he is "under" Jove. Coleridge too stopped just short of the declaration that the poet is the unacknowledged creator of the universe. In the context of a tribute to Wordsworth, he wrote to Richard Sharp that

> . . . Imagination or the *modifying* Power in that highest sense of the word in which I have ventured to oppose it to Fancy, or the *aggregating* Power . . . is a dim Analogue of Creation, not all that we can *believe* but all that we can *conceive* of creation.[10]

It is interesting to consider Coleridge's theory of the imagination in connection with the effort to participate in divinity as well as in connection with the polarized fantasies—male and female —that kept him in tension. Despite his awareness of and interest in the influence of unconscious material on the poetic act, in the

Biographia Literaria he insists almost compulsively on the superiority of the active faculty of the mind over the passive faculty. It is in fact the inability of the Hartley system of association to account for or even to allow for this active faculty that is at the bottom of his quarrel with it.[11] This insistence on the force of the active faculty of the mind, the formulation of the dynamic secondary imagination as "co-existent with the conscious will,"[12] in the face of everything he knew about the value of passive recall, free association, and the "aversion of many to know themselves,"[13] seems to be the result of a fear of passivity in himself, the old wish to purge the heart within his heart, which never left him.

Side by side with this fear—which masks the wish to be passive—is of course the other fear: the fear of the active faculty—which masks the wish to usurp the father. The conflict between the two fears—or wishes—underlies his metaphysical speculations as it underlies his poetry; and it is precisely the hopeless effort to reconcile them that stimulated his analysis of the mind. In dividing the faculties of the mind and arranging them in a hierarchy, he was once more attempting to sort out the disparate aspects of his own personality. The difficulty was that it would have been impossible for him to follow closely these metaphysically rebellious thoughts without feelings of intense guilt, since they parallel so precisely his own fantasies of usurpation of the father. The result is a fully muddled set of conclusions, which he arrived at in order to pacify what he would have referred to as reason but which may be psychoanalytically defined as the superego. Latent bisexuality, with its attendant hatreds, so terrified him that he was compelled to bow in two directions at once, insisting that the poetic imagination was fully active in the sense that Kubla Khan is fully active, while at the same time he quietly compensated for this aggressive claim by means of passive receptivity to the ideas of other people, and also by means of carefully limiting his dangerous Promethean inclinations to a kind of

"justness" that was "under" or submissive to a kind of Jove—
the Christian God.

ii

It is the parallel between the fruits of his "abstruse research" and
his own fantasies that must have attracted him to metaphysics in
the first place and that continued to hold him to it to the end of
his life. He wanted to "be" both male and female, and these un-
acceptably conflicting wishes, which made it impossible for him
to understand himself, stimulated his efforts toward an understanding of epistemology and ontology, in the hope that they
would prove to be instruments for apprehending the nature of
reality, which to him meant always the nature of the self:

> Poor unlucky Metaphysics! and what are they? A single
> sentence expresses the object and thereby the contents
> of this science. Γνῶθι σεαυτόν: et Deum quantum
> licet, et in Deo omnia acibis. Know thyself: and so shalt
> thou know God, as far as is permitted to a creature
> [note the qualification], and in God all things.—
> Surely, there is a strange—nay, rather a too natural—
> aversion in many to know themselves.[14]

The note of forbidden knowledge, struck clearly in the poetry,
sounds again here. It is only to be expected therefore that his
recognition of the value of metaphysics as a means toward understanding and controlling the self—the third instrument he
picked up for the purpose—[15]led him into those "abstruse researches" which he mistakenly thought would engage his intellect without disturbing his emotions:

> . . . I have sought a refuge from bodily pain and
> mismanaged sensibility in abstruse researches, which
> exercised the strength and subtlety of the understanding
> without awakening the feelings of the heart.[16]

In the *Dejection* ode he referred to the "abstruse research" as
though it had actually done what he expected it to do:

For not to think of what I needs must feel,
  But to be still and patient, all I can;
And haply by abstruse research to steal
  From my own nature all the natural man—
  This was my sole resource, my only plan:
Till that which suits a part infects the whole,
And now is almost grown the habit of my soul.[17]

The cost, he felt, of subduing the emotions by means of the intellect, had grown too great; and he assigned the feeling failure of 1802, which was remarkably similar to his feeling failure when he heard about Frank's death in 1793, to a cause that was safely removed from the real trouble: psychic fatigue in the face of unacceptable unconscious wishes.

The fact is that these "researches" could not possibly have engaged his intellect without disturbing his emotions. The effort to arrive at an ontological premise took him perilously close to the precipice where Kant himself had to back away: the heights of independent and lonely self-assertion that were the result of the conviction that existence precedes essence—that man is free not only to assert himself but also to create himself; and in despair, in order to avoid the leap of Empedocles, Coleridge like Montaigne before him took instead the leap of faith.

Even in mid-leap, when Coleridge was engaging in still another reenactment of his reading of the prayer book as a child, in an effort to prove himself a "child of frailty" submissive before God, demonstrating as fully as he could his passive nature, he lit upon a phrase for expressing the godhead that carries *sub rosa* the full weight of his impulse toward assertiveness, usurpation: he called it—without originality, to be sure—"the absolute I AM." Much of the paragraph surrounding the phrase is interesting:

> This principium commune essendi et cognoscendi, as
> subsisting in a WILL, or primary ACT of self-duplication,
> is the mediate or indirect principle of every science;

but it is the immediate and direct principle of the ultimate
science alone, i.e. of transcendental philosophy alone
... In its very idea therefore as a systematic knowledge
of our collective KNOWING, (scientia scientiae) it
involves the necessity of some one highest principle of
knowing, as at once the source and accompanying form
in all particular acts of intellect and perception. This,
it has been shown, can be found only in the act and
evolution of self-consciousness. We are not investigating
an absolute principium essendi; for then, I admit, many
valid objections might be started against our theory;
but an absolute principium cognoscendi. The result of
both the sciences, or their equatorial point, would be
the principle of a total and undivided philosophy ... In
other words, philosophy would pass into religion, and
religion become inclusive of philosophy. We begin
with the I KNOW MYSELF, in order to end with the
absolute I AM. We proceed from the SELF, in order to
lose and find all self in GOD.[18]

The passage begins with the assertion of the will, fully capitalized, a part of the personality which had always Coleridge's
primary attention because his own will—or ego—was frequently
recalcitrant. The emphasis is on action, always difficult for him,
but the "ACT" turns out to be one of "self-duplication," an interesting notion in the light of the intricate and confusing self-
duplication he engaged in in his poetry.[19] Of course the "self-
duplication" here refers to the psychological event which permits
the self to be both subject and object—object only to itself, however: it "never is an object except for itself,"[20] a statement that is
so fully independent that the compliant coming to rest in "the
absolute I AM" is altogether to be expected. The degree of self-
containment expressed in this "ACT of self-duplication," furthermore, appears to support the conclusion that Coleridge's double
fantasy resulted in autoeroticism, as expressed for example in
Christabel.

The value of epistemology for him is clearly shown in his capitalization of the word "KNOWING;" and it is borne out by his contention that being and knowing are inseparable. The ways of knowing fascinate the man whose knowledge is tabu, partly because his forbidden knowledge exists obsessionally and partly because the guilt it stimulates requires inquiry into the origin of such knowledge. Coleridge's guilt produced a retreat from an absolute principle of existence; it was impossible for him to push his rebellious metaphysics to the conclusion that man exists independently and absolutely: "We are not investigating an absolute principium essendi; for then, I admit, many valid objections might be started against our theory." But an absolute principle of knowing he found undeniable; and linking this principle to the principle of existence gave him the ontological premise he needed—one that could lead directly to the "child of frailty" submissive before the "absolute I AM." It is as though in this part of the *Biographia Literaria* he found it necessary to return to the pantheistic speculations of *The Aeolian Harp*,[21] which had apparently produced enough anxiety in him to stimulate the overt apology to his wife that is expressed in that poem,[22] and to reiterate those speculations with the appearance of meticulous logic and in still another effort to make himself not simply numinous, as he did in *Kubla Khan*, but "justly" numinous, "under" God, exactly as he did when he read his prayer book after running away from home as a child.

The whole passage expresses as directly as possible Coleridge's efforts to participate in divinity—which should be taken to mean efforts at usurpation—and his simultaneous retreat from such efforts; and it expresses beneath these efforts the conflicting male and female wishes that underlie all his behavior and all his work.

iii

It is not surprising that in the *Dejection* ode, the work of a man whose oedipal tensions were so acute and so distorted, there are

signs of metaphysical distress. The connection between monotheism and the oedipal situation is that both produce a powerful
need to search for the father. In both patterns the father is missing, or at the very least elusive, because he exists on an alien
plane of being which it is either heresy—in the case of monotheism—or tabu—in the case of the oedipal situation—for a man
to reach. The emotional substructure of monotheism *is* the oedipal situation; and in the *Dejection* ode Coleridge returned to the
elaborative element of Christian grace that had been useful to
him in the *Rime of the Ancient Mariner*, and to the story of paradise lost that had been useful to him in all the poems that have
been looked at so far.

The passage beginning "There was a time" is a replica, in
small, of the universal need to invent a golden age, to refer, in
the face of an indifferent world—which is to say a world without
the father—to a lost period of grace; and implicit in such a need
is the sense that the loss of grace is deserved. The mood is one of
depression and failure.

Lionel Trilling, in a discussion of Matthew Arnold's *Empedocles on Etna*, writes an interesting paragraph on poems of depression:

> The 18th century would have called Empedocles'
> complaint the spleen—a complaint of Yahoos, Swift
> tells us, and with a prophetic touch of the 19th century
> Swift assures us that its only cure is hard work. The
> Middle Ages called the same malady *acedia* and the
> 19th century spoke of it as the *anhedonia* which William
> James analyzed, the *ennui* which Tolstoi called a desire
> for desires, the *noia* in which Leopardi lived. But
> although this complaint is not wholly generated by
> philosophy—for the psychiatrist has recognized it as a
> classic symptom of neurosis—yet, whatever its psycho-
> biologic basis, it is certainly fostered, encouraged and
> given content by the sufferer's intellectual milieu.

Basic to all its expressions is the sense of failure, of
helplessness, friendlessness, pointlessness . . . John Stuart
Mill describes his state of mind at the crisis in his own
mental history as similar to that of Methodists when
they are smitten with the "conviction of sin;" but the
question which Mill asked himself and the answer he
made, which precipitated and fixed the psychological
mood, were philosophical. "Suppose that all your
objects in life were realized," Mill said; "that all the
changes in institutions and opinions which you are
looking forward to, could be completely affected [sic]
at this very instant: would this be a great joy and
happiness to you?" To the question "an irrepressible
self-consciousness distinctly answered "No!" and months
of despair followed . . . Significantly enough, Mill can
best communicate the nature of his misery by quoting
from Coleridge's "Dejection: An Ode;" the "pain
without a pang, void, dark and drear" which Coleridge
speaks of had followed upon the loss of his own power
of imagination . . . The moods of dejection, of emotional
stoppage, which in a simpler religious age would have
been taken to mean an abandonment by God, in this
age of conflict between religion and science are found
to stem from the misery of living in a pointless universe
which makes pointless everything in it.[23]

Despite its general clearsightedness, Trilling's paragraph puts
a bit too much emphasis on the "intellectual milieu;" Mill's question might have been, as he says, philosophical, but no one who
has read the *Autobiography* will doubt either that the motive for
asking the question was psychological or that there was tension
between Mill and his father. But Trilling's observation that
Mill's quotation of the *Dejection* ode was made "significantly
enough" is extremely suggestive. The significance is that Mill describes his own depression by comparing it both to the "conviction of sin" and to the *Dejection* ode. For both Mill and Cole-

ridge, as for all depressives, the "conviction of sin" arises from guilt in the face of unacknowledged and undischarged aggressions; and the paralysis—of feeling as well as action—that characterizes depression arises from the massive diversion of psychic energy to the process of repression, so that very little energy is left over for interaction with the outer world.

As for the influence of Coleridge's "intellectual milieu" on the disturbance that helped to produce the *Dejection* ode, Coleridge himself believed that it was strong, as we know from his letter to Southey "regretting the loss [of his poetic power], which I attribute to my long and exceedingly severe metaphysical investigations;" but he blames also "ill health, and . . . private afflictions which rendered any subjects immediately connected with feeling a source of pain and disquiet to me."[24] The only way to untie this knot is to understand that the metaphysical investigations, and the ill health, and the private afflictions were all "subjects immediately connected with feeling" for Coleridge and that they were on that account all equally "a source of pain and disquiet" to him.

The reason for the pain and disquiet in the presence of "any subjects immediately connected with feeling" appears to be that Coleridge lacked the ego mobility that would have permitted him to slide freely between fantasy and reality. His trips to the deep well had always been dangerous; of the four poems that give him distinction, *Christabel* and *Kubla Khan* had to be hidden away for almost twenty years, allegedly unfinished, the *Rime of the Ancient Mariner* was finished because of its uniquely suitable elaborative device, and the *Dejection* ode was finished because in it he was able to renounce the disturbing process of poetry-making. The dreams show that the lack of ego mobility produced terror to the point of somatic disturbance, that the fantasy material existed for him always threateningly close to consciousness. The imagery of doors and gates in the poetry, frequently in an ambience of fear,[25] is another indication, in addi-

tion to indications in the dreams, of his difficulty in distinguish-
ing between inner and outer reality, which is what ego mobility
amounts to.

It might be pointed out that the "abstruse research" did not
end with the *Dejection* ode; and that if this research had been as
productive of guilty discomfort as I have said it was, Coleridge
would have found it necessary to give up this pursuit as well as
the pursuit of poetry. In answer to this theoretical objection, it
should be said that discursive prose speculations offered far less
danger of self-exposure, even in his efforts at psychological insight, since prose is more easily kept under control by the active
faculty of the mind which Coleridge was always at such pains to
dignify. And although the development of his philosophical and
aesthetic thought took him through the threatening pathways of
metaphysical rebelliousness, he was always able, in the instrument of prose, to assert and to reiterate the strength of his religious faith and to reconcile it, sometimes with ingenious soph-
istry, with his travels up those pathways.

That he never succeeded inwardly in this reconciliation, any
more than he succeeded in reconciling his unconscious tensions,
is obvious from his continued addiction to laudanum throughout
his life. I have said nothing about drug addiction so far; but at
this point I should like to insist against writers who see it as a
cause rather than a result of his difficulties.[26] Science has come a
long way from De Quincey; it has demonstrated that the value
of opiates is in their power to depress the mind to a point where
unconscious material becomes less threatening. Opiate addiction
is also one kind of oral gratification that passive personalities are
drawn to; Coleridge's hungry recollection of "sops in the pan &
pieces of bread & butter with sugar on them" which in childhood
Frank had and he had not, and the longing for the maternal
"milk of Paradise" that is expressed in *Kubla Khan*, as well as all
the evidence in the poetry that shows the infantile nature of his
imagined Eden, and the evidence in the letters that shows the in-

fantile nature of his relationships with other people, make it clear that it was the sucking pleasure required by the passive side of his nature which made the laudanum bottle irresistible to him.

iv

By the time Coleridge came to write the first draft of *Dejection* in the form of a verse letter ostensibly addressed to Sara Hutchinson, his unconscious tensions and the guilt they caused had created in him his most self-destructive mood, a projection toward himself of the rallying of aggressions that made him more destructive than he had ever been toward others. He had entered his third[27] and most intense period of dejection, a period so painful that in order to survive he found it necessary to discontinue the literary elaboration of his conflicts.

A Letter to—— was composed on April 4, 1802, and its most noticeable theme is the contrast between his wretched marriage and his happiness in the presence of William and Dorothy Wordsworth and Sara and Mary Hutchinson. Bad as the marriage must have been, it began to reach an intolerable level only after Coleridge had "leaped into friendship"[28] with the Wordsworths and the Hutchinsons. By the early part of 1802, several aspects of his life had combined to threaten seriously his always precarious equilibrium. The friendship with the Wordsworths, which had begun to show signs of deterioration in 1800, by 1802 became hopelessly oppressive. De Selincourt, for example, writes of the "contrast in their [Wordsworth's and Coleridge's] fortunes" and goes on to say that Coleridge felt that it was already

> evident in their respective poetic achievements. For he believed with no less conviction than Wordsworth that "the deep power of joy" was alike the inspiration and the true basis of all sane imaginative art. Wordsworth, despite the troubles and anxieties of his life, was essentially "a happy man and therefore bold to look on painful things": [Such a diagnosis of Wordsworth

might be seriously questioned.] of Coleridge he remarked
years later, "It was poor dear Coleridge's constant
infelicity that prevented him from being the poet that
Nature had given him the power to be. He had always
too much personal and domestic discontent to paint
the sorrows of mankind. He could not afford to suffer
with those whom he saw suffer." This is but a restatement
of the view maintained by Coleridge himself in many
of his letters no less than in the *Ode*. He was broken
by "afflictions which rendered any subjects immediately
connected with feeling a source of pain and disquiet
to me," and "when a man is unhappy he writes damned
bad poetry"; or, probably, if he is also a good critic,
he will not write at all. Hence, he feels, while his friend
will go on from strength to strength, he is himself
doomed to poetic sterility.[29]

De Selincourt proceeds to make the point that ". . . this contrast between Wordsworth and himself becomes the root idea of
Dejection." What should be taken account of here is the powerful animosity such a contrast must have stirred up in Coleridge,
side by side with an equally powerful need to deny such animosity by means of protestations of affection. Unfortunately for
Wordsworth, he was two years older than Coleridge and fell
easily into the role of father surrogate that Coleridge had also
attempted to assign to Frank, George, Southey, and Poole. How
far the "contrast in their fortunes" was deliberately if unconsciously created by Coleridge might be gauged by the recollection
that rivalry was for him inextricable from male friendship and
was at the same time so dangerous to him that he had always to
back away from any contest.

In addition to Coleridge's discomfort in his relationship with
Wordsworth, his feelings for Sara Hutchinson—and their recip-
rocation—had grown to the point where it must have been plain
to him that the dreaded heart within his heart was within objective reach. What was called for, obviously, was full masculine

behavior; wretchedness at home and bliss abroad would have presented a clear set of alternatives to a man who was actually feeling what De Selincourt referred to as "the deepest and most permanent passion of his life."[30] But even his overt behavior—let alone the submerged attitudes revealed in his dreams and letters—argues against such an interpretation of Coleridge's feelings for Sara. Between his first meeting with her—four years after his marriage—and the composition of what was to become the first draft of *Dejection* almost three years elapsed. Apologists for his failure to take steps will point out his disapproval of divorce and his repeated professions of love for his children from whom he apparently could not bear to be separated. But the most elementary insight is enough to understand that these reasons are classic rationalizations of an unexpressed and unrecognized reluctance to leave one woman for another; and such an understanding is borne out by the fact that in 1806[31] Coleridge did separate himself from his wife—and his children—without the divorce that would permit him to marry Sara Hutchinson. The objective circumstances fully support the thesis under argument here: that Coleridge not only approached and enacted his marriage to Sarah Fricker with feelings of fear and hostility that prevented its success but that he also suffered unconsciously from fear and a strong revulsion when faced with the prospect of intimacy with any woman whatsoever, no matter how ostensibly beloved she may have appeared to him.

For that matter, even a friend's intimacy with a woman was repugnant to him. The rage that animated his ten-page farewell letter to Southey in 1795, coincident with Southey's prospective marriage to Edith Fricker, has to be recalled in connection with the events early in 1802 involving Wordsworth with Annette Vallon and Mary Hutchinson.[32] Between January 26, 1802, and the date of the composition of *Dejection*, Wordsworth—and Dorothy—were in correspondence with Annette, Mary, and Coleridge.[33] Whalley makes an interesting speculation:[34]

> On 27 January Wordsworth wrote to Annette Vallon—
> possibly announcing his intention of marrying Mary
> Hutchinson. He had evidently received word from
> Annette through a refugee who got into touch with
> Coleridge in London . . . While [Coleridge] was in
> London [on one of his trial separations from his wife]
> he had . . . acted as intermediary in establishing
> communications between Annette and Wordsworth.[35]

Apparently Wordsworth's Franco-British conflict was a whirl-
pool that drew not only Dorothy but Coleridge as well into its
vortex. Various aspects of the conflict undoubtedly contributed
to the distress that Coleridge was suffering from when he wrote
his long verse letter on April 4.

One aspect must have been Wordsworth's confidences to him
concerning the love affair with Annette, to which Coleridge certainly must have reacted very much as Dorothy did.[36] His conflicted feelings for Wordsworth—rivalry and its mask of love—
surely made his role of go-between extremely painful; and the
pain must have been increased and complicated by his awareness
that Wordsworth—like Southey before him—had engaged in a
repulsive heterosexual alliance. In both cases—Southey's and
Wordsworth's—what troubled Coleridge, among other things,
was the degree to which he identified with his friends, much as
a son identifies with his father: it is on this level that the loathing
he felt can be explained. In addition, the presence of yet another
rival (Dorothy, like his mother, would have been a prior rival)
for the affections of Wordsworth as father would be troublesome.

But the most stunning blow of all was delivered by the knowledge that Wordsworth was attempting to reach an agreement
with Annette in order to be free to marry the sister of the woman
with whom Coleridge believed himself to be in love.[37] This was
an assault on several fronts. In the first place, the intense identification with Wordsworth would have produced two effects: one

effect had to be envy of Wordsworth's ability to marry a woman so closely associated for Coleridge with Sara Hutchinson. In this connection Wordsworth takes on all the color of Kubla Khan, who "can" while Coleridge "cannot." The other effect, simultaneous with the first, had to be the stirring up in Coleridge of his own feelings of fear and anger and revulsion toward both men and women. Unfortunately for Coleridge, he found himself in an objective situation that parallelled precisely the fantasy situation he had created in *Kubla Khan*: envy and fear of the primal situation of love between the parents, with all the attendant jealousies and threats—directed toward and imagined from both parents.

The problem of who the recipient of the long verse letter of April 4 actually was can be resolved only by understanding that Coleridge himself could not possibly have resolved it. The reason for his backing and filling in identifying the object—or objects —of the feelings in the letter is that in its primitive form *Dejection* is a farewell not only to poetry-making but also to Wordsworth and, in characteristic fear of his own masculinity and what its expression might do to a love object, to his rival-father, and to himself, it is a farewell to Sara Hutchinson. Again, Coleridge was reading his prayer book in an effort to prove himself docile and therefore harmless. His failure to leave Sarah Fricker Coleridge for Sara Hutchinson, whom he professed to love, was a retreat exactly like the retreat from Mary Evans, who he was afraid would "effeminate [his] intellect."

All the circumstances of Coleridge's life, during the period just preceding the composition of *A Letter to——*, combined with ironic harmony to produce in him the climate of despair. His "abstruse research," since it led him toward a dangerous Promethean position, reanimated old fears from which he had to retreat to an attitude of prayer like Christabel's. The obvious comparisons to be made between himself and Wordsworth excited again the atmosphere of rivalry that underlies *Kubla Khan*.

And the increasing responsiveness of Sara Hutchinson invited him to the role of the demon-lover. All three areas of his life— metaphysics, friendship, and love—simultaneously appeared threatening to him because they were full of the temptation to virility. His response to the temptation was the long verse letter that ostensibly pleads sorrow, paralysis, and piety.

7. The First Draft of *Dejection*: An Explication

*One excellent use of communication of Sorrows to a
Friend is this: that in relating what ails us we ourselves
first know exactly what the real Grief is—& see it for
itself, in its own form & limits—Unspoken Grief is a
misty medley, of which the real affliction only plays
the first fiddle—blows the Horn, to a scattered mob of
obscure feelings &c. Perhaps, at certain moments a
single almost insignificant Sorrow may, by association,
bring together all the little relicts of pain & discomfort,
bodily & mental, that we have endured even from
Infancy.*—Coleridge

A Letter to—— begins, as the received version of the *Dejection*
ode begins, with a reference to an old ballad, but without the
epigraph which in the final version makes it clear that the ballad
is in control of the poem.

Well! if the Bard was weatherwise, who made
The grand old Ballad of Sir Patrick Spence,
This Night, so tranquil now, will not go hence
Unrous'd by winds, that ply a busier trade
Than that, which moulds yon clouds in lazy flakes,
Or the dull sobbing Draft, that drones & rakes
Upon the Strings of this Eolian Lute,
　　Which better far were mute.
　　For, lo! the New Moon, winter-bright!
And [*all-suffus'd*] overspread with phantom Light,

119

(With swimming phantom Light o'erspread
But rimm'd & circled with a silver Thread)
I see the Old Moon in her Lap, foretelling
The coming-on of Rain & squally Blast—
O! Sara! that the Gust ev'n now were swelling,
And the slant Night-shower driving loud & fast![1]

The first sixteen lines begin with an apparent fear of the prospect of stormy winds—"winds, that ply a busier trade"—that
would be destructive for the persona. From fear the lines move to
an apparent welcome of self-destruction: ". . . this Eolian Lute,/
Which better far were mute." Eventually, the passage presents a
fully expressed longing for the storm: "O! Sara! that the Gust
ev'n now were swelling,/ And the slant Night-shower driving
loud & fast!"

The presence of fear in the passage may not readily be seen
unless the reference to the ballad is taken into account. The reference is to "The grand old Ballad of Sir Patrick Spence," and it
is amplified by the image of the "New Moon . . . [with] the Old
Moon in her Lap,[2] foretelling/ The coming-on of Rain & squally
Blast." In the ballad, a member of Sir Patrick's crew interprets
the sight of "the new moone/ Wi' the auld moone in hir arme"[3]
as an omen of "harme;" and his fears are entirely borne out:

O our Scots nobles wer richt laith
    To weet their cork-heild schoone;
Bot lang owre a' the play wer playd,
    Thair hats they swam aboone.

It is easy to see why the ballad of Sir Patrick Spence attracted
Coleridge. The narrative expresses fully his fantasies of usurpation and punishment. Sir Patrick, "the best sailor," is commanded
to sail the king's ship[4] upon the sea in weather which both Patrick
and his crew know is fatal to navigators; in other words, the king
(the father), in giving such an order, is inviting usurpation, pre-
senting temptation to virility, but at the price of certain death.
The first descriptive detail prepares the reader for the punitive

nature of the king: he is "Drinking the blude-reid wine"—a euphemistic revision of the blood that ogres habitually drink in
fairy and folk tales. Behind the command of the king is the
usurper's own fantasy, conveniently displaced onto the punitive
father, as if the act of usurpation were not a matter of individual
responsibility but rather an inevitable necessity like the prophecy
that King Oedipus and other figures in Greek myth are ostensibly forced to fulfill.

The command terrifies Sir Patrick, and at the second line of
the king's letter "The teir blinded his ee;" already, in mere prospect, he is victim of the most fitting punishment for usurpation,
like Coleridge in his dream and like King Oedipus and Teiresias:
he is blinded, if only by a euphemistic tear. Sir Patrick does not
resort to projections as remote as Destiny, but pins the blame
exactly where Coleridge would unconsciously have pinned it—
on the father, in the person of the king:

> O quha is this has don this deid,
>> This ill deid don to me;
> To send me out this time o'the yeir,
>> To sail upon the se?

There is blame also for the mother, in the punishment that is
inflicted on her by means of multiplication and displacement in
the stanzas detailing the waiting grief of the ladies, who will see
their own dear lords "na mair." As a matter of fact, in the ballad
as for Coleridge, the mother comes off far worse than the father,
who is not referred to at all after the stanza that complains of his
cruelty.[5] Besides providing punishment for the mother, the
stanzas that describe the ladies also fall in neatly with Coleridge's
penchant for self-pity—a natural coincidence since self-pity is
always a mask of aggressions.

But the most radiant detail for Coleridge would have been
the omen of death as interpreted by one of the crew: "the new
moone/ Wi' the auld moone in hir arme." As a compression of
the *liebestod* drama that dominated his fantasies, this image is

exquisitely appropriate; it expresses everything for him. The fear and guilt that attend the vision of usurpation would interpret this image as an omen of death-in-life, correspondent to the punishment of the mariner in the *Rime* as well as to comparable details in Coleridge's dreams and in his other poems, as life (the new moon) is seen to contain death (the old moon) and as love (the new moon) holds death (the old moon) in her embrace. The whole complex of two moons is, besides, a variation of the image of the child in the lap (a variation which Coleridge established by changing the ballad's phraseology when he came to write *A Letter to*——), with the child's youth disguised by the adjective *auld*, and with the possibility that the "new moone" could represent, in spite of the feminine pronoun, the mother or the father. Reading the adjective *auld* as a disguise, furthermore, would have reminded Coleridge unconsciously that his childhood fantasies were not childlike but that they were fed by sexual aggression directed, it must be assumed on the basis of everything that has been said up to this point about Coleridge's latent bisexuality, toward both parents.

Without such elaborative interpretation, the image is a stark picture of the female moon with the literally old moon in her embrace, which must have suggested to Coleridge (and perhaps to the devisers and perpetuators of the ballad as well) that if the new moon is female, the old moon must be male, especially as old age is a common attribute of the fantasied father. The omen of death in the ballad, then, is again a representation of the primal scene, the sight of which, real or imagined, calls for punishment not only by blindness/castration but also by death. Another possible interpretation for Coleridge would have been that the new moon, embracing the old one, represented his retaliatory wish for the death of the phallic mother. Simultaneous with this wish was perhaps the notion that the primal embrace killed the father, a notion that the ballad makers may perhaps also have held since the king disappears in the ballad.

Sir Patrick's punishment of death by water, together with his whole crew (the persona multiplied), recalls of course the near-drowning of the mariner in the *Rime*; and even the reason for the mariner's punishment is echoed in the ballad: both Sir Patrick and the mariner are witnesses of the primal scene. And the setting of both narratives is, fittingly, the sea: the element of sexuality itself, with its dangerous and uncharted areas beyond the boundaries that are fixed by tabus. The source and nature of all Coleridge's guilts—the experience of the primal scene—were surely assaulted by "the grand old Ballad of Sir Patrick Spence;" and in the moment when his mood of self-pity and self-destruction was masking his most powerful feelings of aggression, it is no wonder that his unconscious need for punishment pushed him to the choice of this ballad as the animating impulse behind *A Letter to——*.

ii

The mood of the first sixteen lines of *A Letter to——* is suicidal, a state of mind resulting from the guilt that attends forbidden knowledge as symbolized by the image of the two moons. But it is not clear whether the persona wishes the quietus made by himself or by someone else. The passage establishes a direct relationship between the external wind of the threatening storm and the internal "Eolian Lute" which is a metaphor for the passive self; and in the whole hierarchy of winds set up in the first eight lines —those "that ply a busier trade" (storm winds), "that, which moulds yon clouds in lazy flakes," and "the dull sobbing Draft" —there is not one that can be confronted, let alone dominated, by the self. So far, it looks as though destruction is expected at the hands of something or someone in the external world. Line eight, which is the first suicidal expression in the poem, asserts that it would be "better far" if the Eolian Lute were "mute"— an assertion that carries more than one implication. In the first place, it suggests that the writer knows that it would be "better

far" for him not to say what he is about to say; in other words, he
has reservations about expressing the impulses he is feeling, since
they are aggressive and also perhaps too revealing of himself.
In the second place, it suggests that it would be "better far" if
the passive self—the Eolian Lute—were not functioning at all,
which is to say that it would be "better far" if he—or his passive
self—were dead. In the context of winds established so far, the
muteness, or death, of the self, would have to be brought about
by the threatening storm winds, which could of course destroy a
lute. The two implications of the eighth line are inextricable in
a causal relationship; he wishes he were dead because of what he
is feeling. And he looks for destruction from the outside because
his aggressive feelings make it necessary for the passive mask to
take over, as it habitually did for him, to make him appear harmless. In a mood like this, suicide would be too aggressive; it would
be an act, after all, and an act is precisely what Coleridge did
not dare to perform, and what his repressions did not leave him
enough energy for. But paradoxically, it is the passive part of the
self that he wishes were dead: the expression here is another variation of the wish to purge himself of his passive, female needs,
the heart within the heart; and it points also toward his fantasies
of destructive sexual behavior toward women. He would have
liked to be both demon-lover and woman wailing for him. So
that the whole passage, before line nine, indicates not a simple
passive death wish but powerfully conflicted wishes for both passivity and assertion, which find a kind of resolution here in the
idea of death—the only mode in which both these terrifying possibilities could be overcome.

The omen that signals death in the ballad of Sir Patrick Spence
appears in the second eight lines. It is introduced by the conjunction *for*, with the implication that it would be better for the lute
to be destroyed *because* this omen appears. The logic here is im-
peccable; the writer sees a representation of the primal scene and
therefore feels he ought to be punished. The first of the relatively

few emendations in the *Letter* occurs in the first description of
the omen:

> ... the New Moon, winter-bright!
> And [*all-suffus'd*] overspread with phantom Light,

In all of the first sixteen lines, this is the only emendation, and it
is an indication that Coleridge had some discomfort in producing
the image. It seems likely that *overspread* superseded *all-suffus'd*
because of the connotations of liquid that attach to the phrase he
struck out, and not simply because *overspread* could be con-
tracted for purposes of repetition in deference to the ballad form.
He could not avoid the association of liquid, however, even—or
perhaps particularly—while he was making this female new
moon numinous, a mother-goddess; he repeated *phantom light*
and made it *swimming*. In this synesthetic perception of "phantom light" that is "swimming" there is a suggestion that sexuality
itself—represented by water—is holy, or tabu, much in the same
way that the persona of *Kubla Khan* becomes holy and terrifying at the end of that poem, because of his forbidden sexual
knowledge.

Appropriately, this water-drenched image prepares for "The
coming-on of Rain & squally Blast;" and the stanza ends with
a strongly expressed wish that raises the possibility that what the
writer longed for was not only death from an external source but
also the power to bring death on himself. It is at this point that
the confusion concerning the source of destruction is at its peak:

> O! Sara! that the Gust ev'n now were swelling,
> And the slant Night-shower driving loud & fast!

Whether you read these lines as addressed to a woman or to a
man, their sexual connotations are clear; and in either case, since
both the "Gust" and the "slant Night-shower" proceed from the
fountain of the destructive storm, it is apparent that wishing for
his own sexual release meant to him also wishing for his death.
If he were to behave in a fully masculine way, the result—be-

cause of his guilt—could only be punishment by death. Read in this way, the stanza proceeds toward an equation of the external storm with the interior storm created by his own punitive super-ego, an equation that is fully borne out in the next stanza, which overtly presents the writer's emotional state as a parallel to the tranquil night before the storm, "unrous'd by winds." But if you read the last two lines of the first stanza as addressed to a man (substitute William or Thomas for Sara), then the longing could also be interpreted as a wish to be punished by the full sexuality of the father, *or* as a wish to punish the father by means of sexual aggression. The density of these two lines, which point in several directions at once, is more easily understood if their meaning is simplified into two generalizations: that the oedipal situation necessarily makes the son feel both dangerous and in danger, and that a distorted oedipal situation like Coleridge's made him feel dangerous toward and in danger of retaliation from both the father and the mother.

The result of such a threatening dilemma is precisely the "Grief without a pang, void, dark, & drear," of the second stanza. The import of lines seventeen through forty-three is simply that the writer is unable to feel anything. The feeling failure is ex-pressed in the poem immediately after the wish for the swelling "Gust" and the "slant Night-shower" that reveals the dilemma of unacceptable and conflicting impulses; the necessity to make himself unable to feel these impulses brings about paralysis.

iii

In the second stanza the "Grief without a pang" is defined in sev-eral ways, all of which more or less plainly refer not only to the general paralysis of feeling but also to the specific paralysis of the writer's sexual power. It is

A stifling, drowsy, unimpassion'd Grief
That finds no natural Outlet, no Relief
In word, or sigh, or tear.

Word, sigh, and tear are all substitutes for sexual release; the writer claims he can find none of them. And yet, in the very act of writing this long verse letter he was finding all too many words to substitute for such release and to represent sigh and tear as well: the whole poem is, like his addiction to opium, a form of oral gratification demanded by his essentially undeveloped sexuality.

One reason he protests that this "Grief" cannot find word, sigh, or tear, is that he wishes to deny what he wants to say. The hesitation in prospect of expressing himself at all in the poem is noticeable in the first stanza in the declaration that the Eolian Lute ought to be mute; and in the second stanza the hesitation is rationalized by means of the declaration that he really cannot say the word or sigh the sigh or weep the tear that would express his feelings and relieve him. Again, he is saying his prayers in the face of his own aggressions. But another reason for his declared failure to find word, sigh, or tear, is his half-conscious awareness that what he is saying or about to say is not an overt expression of the deep truth about himself and others. In addition, and perhaps strongest of all, is the implication that if he says he cannot find word, sigh, or tear, and yet is plainly finding them, then word, sigh, or tear, must be not what he misses but only a disguise for what he misses. The relief he wants is not to be had by these means.

He calls his state of mind a "heartless Mood," by which he means apparently that he has no heart with which to feel; but in the light of the latent aggressions in the poem the word *heartless* can be taken also to mean exactly what it does in normal usage. In such a mood he finds himself wooed by a "Throstle"

> That pipes within the Larch tree, not unseen,
> (The Larch, which pushes out in tassels green
> It's bundled Leafits) woo'd to mild Delights
> By all the tender Sounds & gentle Sights
> Of this sweet Primrose-month—& *vainly* woo'd.

Those italics are Coleridge's, although if he had not put them there they would have had to be invented. Behind the recipient of this poem is the sexually undifferentiated parent of Coleridge's childhood. He is wooed by the throstle but the throstle is in a tree and the image of the tree is repeated, the second time with an apparently irrelevant detail: it "pushes out in tassels green/ It's bundled Leafits" so that it looks something like the tree under which Christabel prays. The tree in *Christabel* has mistletoe and this one has "tassels [of] bundled Leafits;" both are drawn with male sexual adornments. It is no surprise then to find Coleridge saying that he is wooed by the bird but that he is *vainly* wooed, just as he had been vainly wooed (if at all) by Mary Evans, and as he would in a few months be vainly wooed in a dream by the "frightful pale woman of a gigantic Height, who I thought wanted to kiss me." Of Mary Evans he had been afraid because she might have "effeminated" his intellect; the women in his dreams are phallic women and they also have powers of castration and/or destruction. The throstle that woos him here, in its juxtaposition with the ornamental tree, is still another potentially castrating seducer, a phallic woman; and it *vainly* woos him because he is terrified of it. A sexual encounter with any woman was a prospect that always called up in him the need to deny his own sexuality by clinging to the pose of the child of frailty.

If it is assumed that this verse letter was intended for Sara Hutchinson, then the insistence on the futility of seduction is certainly a far cry from an expression of love for her, which many writers have taken it to be. Characteristically, he follows this refusal of seduction by an affectionate superlative, as if to deny what he has just expressed:

O dearest Sara!

But then he goes back to the subject of his feeling failure and develops it with some interesting details:

. . . in this heartless Mood
All this long Eve, so balmy & serene,

Have I been gazing on the western Sky
And it's peculiar Tint of Yellow Green—
And still I gaze—& with how blank an eye!
And those thin Clouds above, in flakes & bars,
That give away their Motion to the Stars;
Those Stars, that glide behind them, or between,
Now sparkling, now bedimm'd, but always seen;
Yon crescent Moon, as fix'd as if it grew
In it's own cloudless, starless Lake of Blue—
A boat becalm'd! dear William's Sky Canoe!
—I see them all, so excellently fair!
I see, not feel, how beautiful they are.

Here the emphasis is on the eye and on seeing; the regret that the writer gazes "with how blank an eye" must be read as regret that like the persona in *Kubla Khan* he "cannot," he is unable to behave as a man: the primitive equation of the eye and the genitalia is certainly operative here as it is in his dreams and his other poems. The defective "eye" sees reality incoherently:

... those thin Clouds above, in flakes & bars,
That give away their Motion to the Stars;
Those Stars, that glide behind them, or between.

As naturalistic detail, the movement of the stars is impossible; and the writer knows it. It is as though he were calling attention to his defective vision by emphasizing the phenomenon of optical illusion. Furthermore, in the presence of powerful emotions like the ones he is feeling, his guilt and fear would be likely to produce a profound mistrust of the stability of his own identity, and it is this distrust that is projected onto the stars which seem to move when they are in fact not moving.

But one star is fixed—

Yon crescent Moon, as fix'd as if it grew
In it's own cloudless, starless Lake of Blue—

so that the only certainty to be found in this illusory landscape is the omen of death. The new moon is then defined as "A boat becalm'd" and as "dear William's Sky Canoe," which round out an odd little catalog of associations. The "boat becalm'd," like the becalmed ship in the *Rime of the Ancient Mariner*, connotes death, even though it is presented overtly as something delightful; and "dear William's Sky Canoe," in association with the new moon and the motionless boat, certainly refers to his feelings for Wordsworth, and makes it clear that it is not only seduction by Sara that he fears but also seduction by Wordsworth.

This trio of death omens becomes the climactic antecedent of the concluding lines of this stanza:

—I see them all, so excellently fair!
I see, not feel, how beautiful they are.

The lines are truer than Coleridge knew. Like the two lines that conclude stanza one, they are extremely dense with meaning. First, he does indeed "see them all, so excellently fair;" he is attracted to death. Second, all three of these images represent incest wishes. The new moon of course represents the mother; the "boat becalm'd" represents his passive self which would be intimate with the father; and "dear William's Sky Canoe" represents the father. Third, he cannot feel their beauty, even though he sees it, because the powerful tabus set up by his superego have diverted so much of his psychic energy from feeling to repression.

The climate of the second stanza, in which the writer creates a parallel between the quiet evening before the storm and his own absence of feeling, fully expresses these ambivalent incest wishes. "A Grief without a pang . . ./ That finds no natural Outlet, no Relief," is feeling failure and more; it is also Tolstoi's "desire for desires," with the obvious sexual connotations. But it is in addition a failure of receptivity. As it finds no outlet (in the same way that the night is swollen), neither has it any inlet by which it can be entered and aroused by the oncoming external storm. This is the despair of the man who, wishing to perform both roles in the sexual drama, finds that as a consequence he can perform neither.

iv

The first stanza of the received version of *Dejection* follows almost exactly the first stanza of *A Letter to*——; the body of the stanza has only a few word changes which either clarify the sense or improve the style. But four lines are added to its conclusion:

> Those sounds which oft have raised me, whilst they awed,
> > And sent my soul abroad,
> Might now perhaps their wonted impulse give,
> Might startle this dull pain, and make it move and live!

The addition has two effects: it raises the distinction between then and now, which by the sixth stanza is revealed to be central to the poem; and it dulls the effect of the two lines that express the wish for the "gust" and the "slant Night-shower driving loud & fast!" The dulling is produced by the description of gust and shower as "sounds"—a weak word—and by the diffusion of the submerged meaning of gust and shower in generalities. On the other hand, the added lines sharpen the expression of the need for punishment, since the longing they express is for pain not pleasure.

Stanza two makes many more changes. There is no reference whatever to the writer's being vainly wooed, only the observation that he is

> . . . in this wan and heartless mood,
> To other thoughts by yonder throstle woo'd.

The ornamental tree, with all its connotations, has disappeared, and along with it the definitions of the moon as "A boat becalm'd" and as "dear William's Sky Canoe." The removal of the notion of being vainly wooed clouds somewhat even the overt meaning of the stanza; the removal of the other images, however, improves the verse, since they are all irrelevant to it. The cancellation of these details undoubtedly proceeded from Coleridge's sense of style, his reluctance to let three words do the work of one; but it is equally certain that the reservations about express-

ing his feelings, apparent in the wish for the lute to be stilled,
were unconsciously at work: the most threatening details of the
stanza have been omitted.[6]

Beginning with stanza three of *A Letter to*———, the differences between the two versions of the poem go wild; there is no
longer the faintest correspondence between the organization of
stanzas in the *Letter* and that in the ode. Stanza three of the *Letter* is preserved in the ode for eight lines, and then begins a passage of a hundred and thirty-one lines in the *Letter* that are
omitted from the received version.

These lines in the letter continue on the subject of the writer's
feeling failure. After the declaration that "My genial Spirits fail,"
followed by the familiar statement that "I may not hope from
outward Forms to win/The Passion & the Life, whose Fountains
are within" (the diction here is notable: it is inner "fountains"
that would produce what he wants—"passion" and "life"),[7] the
writer finds that even the thought of the beloved watching in a
different place the same sky he watches moves him only feebly.

> Feebly! O feebly!—Yet
> (I well remember it)
> In my first Dawn of Youth that Fancy stole
> With many [*gentle*] secret Yearnings on my Soul.
> At eve, sky-gazing in "ecstatic fit"
> (Alas! for cloister'd in a city School
> The Sky was all, I knew, of Beautiful)
> At the barr'd window often did I sit,
> And oft upon the leaded School-roof lay,
>   And to myself would say—
> There does not live the Man so stripp'd of good affections
> As not to love to see a Maiden's quiet Eyes
> Uprais'd, and linking on sweet Dreams by dim
>   Connections
> To Moon, or Evening Star, or glorious western Skies—
> While yet a Boy, this Thought would so pursue me
> That often it became a kind of Vision to me!

The sense of this passage is obscure. The antecedent of "that Fancy," for instance, is far from clear. It appears to be the thought of the absent beloved who perhaps is sharing his sky-watching. But if he is writing to Sara, the beloved—although absent—is a real woman; in his boyhood imagination, apparently, there was no beloved, only the idea of one. The difference between then and now seems to be a strong failure of the imagination which in boyhood could produce feeling without an object but which now cannot do so even with the stimulus of a real, although absent, woman.

This difference at least was undoubtedly genuine. During his friendship with the Evanses he had observed of himself that he had stronger feelings for Mary when he was away from her than he had in her presence; but at this point, his fear had grown so that even the relatively safe daydream had to be repressed. The whole passage of a hundred and thirty-one lines, which he failed to include in the ode, looks like a frantic effort to stimulate feeling in himself by means of the recollection of persons and events which must formerly have stirred in him powerful emotions (although these could not possibly have been what he thought they were); and the more frantic the effort, the less tranquillity, or receptivity to stimuli, he was able to experience.

The emphasis on eyes continues heavily throughout the whole passage, indicating the continuing substructure of sexual associations; it is the "Maiden's quiet Eyes," for example, that he remembers imagining in boyhood; and some lines further on he addresses Sara in the spirit of the Songs of Solomon as "O Sister! O Beloved!" and goes on to

> Those dear wild Eyes,[8] that see
> Even now the Heaven, *I* see—
> There is a Prayer in them! It is for *me*—
> And I, dear Sara—*I* am blessing *thee*!

Considering that this expression of faith in the power of eyes to pray and bless follows a stanza in which he says that

> I guess, that thou has stood
> And watch'd yon Crescent, & it's ghost-like Moon [,]

it is apparent that he means precisely the opposite of what he
says. Sara must also have seen the death omen; therefore they
bless each other. Simple logic requires that the conclusion be revised in order to follow the premise. The "blessing" here is a disguise, by means of contrast, for the curse that the mariner's crew
inflict with their eyes. Immediately after his "guess" that Sara has
seen the death omen, he makes this confession:

> And yet, far rather in my present Mood
> I would, that thou'dst been sitting all this while
> Upon the sod-built Seat of Camomile—

ostensibly a reference to the Sara Seat which Coleridge, Dorothy,
and William had built in a happy mood.[9] But given his "present
Mood" the adjective *sod-built* suggests not joy but death. And in
the context of this verse letter, which goes on to picture Sara as
"belonging" not to Coleridge but to William and Dorothy and
Mary (lines 133-163), his wish makes sense: if she had been "sit-
ting all this while" on the Sara seat, she would have been in some
sense "his," she would have been alone; furthermore, her death
would have been her ultimate removal from his rivals, and it
would also have served his fantasy of retaliatory aggression toward the mother.

It is only after this wish is expressed that he is able to write
that

> I feel my spirit moved—

and to go on with the passage about the "wild Eyes" that pray
and bless. The pattern should be familiar by now; his aggressive
wishes are always immediately followed by the pose of the child
of frailty, usually the resort to prayer.

v

Further evidence of the discrepancy between what the writer expresses and what he intends is presented in the succeeding stanza,

which begins by comparing a "happy night" with Sara and Mary Hutchinson to this evening before the storm:

> It was as calm as this, that happy night
> When Mary, thou, & I together were,
> The low decaying Fire our only Light,
> And listen'd to the stillness of the Air!
> O that affectionate & blameless Maid,
> Dear Mary! on her Lap my head she lay'd—
>   Her Hand was on my Brow,
>   Even as my own is now;
> And on my Cheek I felt [thy][10] eye-lash play.
> Such joy I had, that I may truly say,
> My Spirit was awe-stricken with the Excess
> And trance-like Depth of it's brief Happiness.

It is a question whether this comparison is the result of deliberate irony—the superficial similarity of the two occasions with regard to weather underlining the difference in mood between then and now—or whether the lines express a lapse of concentration that makes the threatening evening seem simply and pleasurably "calm." Either way, the details in the stanza point toward a profound similarity between the events he recalls and his present mood. He had both Sara and Mary alone; he was, for the time being, in the enviable position of Wordsworth in the dream that was to beset him in a few months—flanked by two women. Besides, the occasion brought to actuality his fantasy of the child in the lap: Mary—now engaged to marry Wordsworth—laid his head on her lap. Such a cosy evening (the details of Mary's hand on his brow and Sara's eyelash on his cheek, simultaneously, present a pretty eccentric picture) undoubtedly stimulated his fears and guilts since it enabled him to act out his double fantasy —of usurpation and of passivity—although the event certainly appears to be all too innocuous. It is no wonder that his

> ... Spirit was awe-stricken with the Excess
> And trance-like Depth of it's brief Happiness.

Trance-like it certainly must have been; the whole scene must have given him a profound sense of *déjà-vu.*

There follow several stanzas insisting that his chief concern is for Sara's happiness, a protestation of selflessness that is not always persuasive. Expatiating on his "fair Remembrances," he asks,

> Where were they, Sara?—or did I not strive
> To win them to me?—on the fretting Hour
> Then when I wrote thee that complaining Scroll,
> Which even to bodily Sickness bruis'd thy Soul!
> And yet thou blam'st thyself alone! And yet
>   Forbidd'st me all Regret!
>
> And must I not regret, that I distress'd
> Thee, best belov'd! who lovest me the best?
> My better mind had fled, I know not whither,
> For O! was this an Absent Friend's Employ
> To send from far both Pain & Sorrow thither
>   Where still his Blessings should have call'd down Joy!
> I read thy guileless Letter[11] o'er again—
> I hear thee of thy blameless Self complain—
> And only this I learn—& this, alas! I know—
> That thou art weak & pale with Sickness, Grief & Pain—
>   And *I—I* made thee so!

Such awareness of his own hostile behavior, in the context of a verse letter saturated with submerged hostility, recalls his letter to Southey in which he caught himself up in a self-pitying burst of emotion and rebuked himself but was powerless to write otherwise. His emphasis on the "I" who made Sara suffer looks, like a Janus face, in two directions at once: there is unconscious pride here in his ability to affect her (for the moment he "can" like Kubla Khan), and there is fear and guilt in the sensing of such power.

The next stanza sets Sara in the bosom of the Wordsworth family, apart from him:

O for my own sake I regret perforce
Whatever turns thee, Sara! from the course
Of calm Well-being & a Heart at rest!
When thou, & with thee those, whom thou lov'st best,
Shall dwell together in one happy Home,
One House, the dear *abiding* Home of All,
I too will crown me with a Coronal—
Nor shall this Heart in idle Wishes roam
    Morbidly soft!
No! let me trust, that I shall wear away
In no inglorious Toils the manly Day,
And only now & then, & not too oft,
Some dear & memorable Eve will bless
Dreaming of all your Loves & Quietness.

If there is any doubt that this is a farewell to Sara, among others, these lines that recall his farewell letter to Mary Evans ought to settle it. To Mary he had written:

> To love you Habit has made unalterable. This passion however, divested, as it now is of all Shadow of Hope, [Mary had become engaged to be married] will lose it's disquieting power. Far distant from you I shall journey thro' the vale of Men in calmness. He cannot long be wretched, who dares be actively virtuous.

In both cases he renounced love in favor of work; and the insistence, in both letters, on activity—his resolve to "wear away/ In no inglorious Toils the manly Day," rather than to "roam/ Morbidly soft," and that "He cannot long be wretched, who dares be actively virtuous"—points to his fear of being effeminated in love: of Mary he had written that she would have "effeminated [his] intellect," and it is clear that he was afraid of Sara in the same way: he saw both women as essentially phallic, punitive, and capable of castration.

Sara's alienation from him, therefore, her "belonging" to the Wordsworths, must have been Coleridge's own doing. It could not have been otherwise. In fact the next stanza says as much:

Be happy, & I need thee not in sight.
Peace in thy Heart, & Quiet in thy Dwelling,
Health in thy Limbs, & in thine Eyes the Light
Of Love, & Hope, & honorable Feeling—
Where e'er I am, I shall be well content!
Not near[*ly*] thee, haply shall be more content!

Haply. About his feelings for Mary Evans he had written to
Southey that

When she was present, she was to me only as a very
dear Sister: it was in absence, that I felt those gnawings
of Suspense, and that Dreaminess of Mind, which
evidence an affection more restless, yet scarcely less pure,
than the fraternal.

If Mary Evans was too dangerous for him to feel love when
they were together, Sara Hutchinson, with whom he had gone at
least as far as to let her eyelash touch his cheek,[12] must have been
terrifying. His feeling failure, in the moment of writing the verse
letter, was—at least in part—the result of increased fear brought
about by the greater intimacy he had experienced with Sara than
he had with Mary, so that his efforts to feel, in this letter, could
not possibly have succeeded, as the similar effort in the letter to
Southey did. The value of the change in line 149 from adverb to
adjective is open to speculation. He might have intended "Not
nearly so content as when I am with you;" or he might have intended "Not nearly so content as if you did not live at all." In the
first case, he would have been altering a falsehood to resemble
truth more closely; in the second case, he would have been
weakening a powerful wish. Either way, the change is an indication of agitation beneath the expression, since it is the only
change in the space of a hundred and twenty-one lines; and the
agitation must have proceeded from the pre-conscious awareness
of his animosity toward women in general and toward Sara in
particular. The extravagant apology for having caused Sara pain,
in lines 111-129, is evidence of such pre-conscious awareness.

Rationalization follows the expression of his preference for distance between him and Sara.

> To all things I prefer the Permanent.
> And better seems it for a Heart, like mine,
> Always to *know*, then [sic] sometimes to behold,
>   *Their* happiness & thine—
> For Change doth trouble me with pangs untold!
> To see thee, hear thee, feel thee—then to part!
>   Oh!—it weighs down the Heart!
> To *visit* those, I love, as I love thee,
> Mary, & William, & dear Dorothy,
> It is but a temptation to repine—
> The transientness is Poison in the Wine,
> Eats out the pith of Joy, makes all Joy hollow,
> All Pleasure a dim Dream of Pain to follow!

Pain to follow indeed. It is not transientness that is poison in the wine, but fear and guilt. The only honest observation in the passage is that "Change doth trouble me with pangs untold!" Objectively he could have overcome the transientness; but psychologically, change, for a personality whose ego mobility is deficient, is troublesome: the inability to distinguish between fantasy and reality results in a degree, more or less, of rigidity, and the change he feared was not the change from happiness with Sara Hutchinson to wretchedness with his wife but the change from wretchedness with his wife to happiness with Sara Hutchinson. That he had enough of an impulse toward self-preservation to leave his wife in 1806 undoubtedly saved him from the suicide that his dreams and his poems and the events of his life indicate he was always contemplating; but the impulse was not strong enough for him to leave her and to join the other Sara. Or perhaps it would be better to say that rejecting Sara Hutchinson actually was a result of his impulse toward self-preservation, given the strength of his fantasies which would have made such a union seem to him a dangerous act of male assertion.

The remainder of the hundred and thirty-one lines that do not appear in the ode, except for six lines which powerfully present his wretchedness in marriage in contrast to the happiness he imagines his friends to be enjoying, ostensibly expresses his concern for Sara's well-being and the pain any injury to her would cause him:

> But (let me say it! for I vainly strive
> To beat away the Thought), but if thou pin'd,
> Whate'er the Cause, in body or in mind,
> I were the miserablest Man alive
> To know it & be absent! Thy Delights
> Far off, or near, alike I may partake—
> But O! to mourn for thee, & to forsake
> All power, all hope of giving comfort to thee—
> To know that thou art weak & worn with pain,
> And not to hear thee, Sara! not to view thee—
> > Not sit beside thy Bed
> > Not press thy aching Head,
> > Not bring thee Health again—
> > At least to hope, to try—
> By this Voice, which thou lov'st, & by this earnest Eye—

The passage breaks off, unfinished, in the middle of a sentence, in the middle of a clear intention to swear by his voice and his eye—as though he had some dim awareness that these were defective and that the oath would be perjury in any event—that he would rescue the maiden whose hypothetical distress he so vividly created in words. The whole passage is a pristine example of the pleasure to be found in the distress of a suffering woman, a pleasure that persists beneath any number of romantic rescues.[18]

vi

From this point in the *Letter*, there are correspondences between it and the ode; but large shifts in organization took place before the poem was first published. The *Letter* moves from the unfin-

ished oath directly to what later became the seventh, or penultimate, stanza of the ode. What we have so far is a rough correspondence between stanzas one and two of the two versions, then
a massive flood of emotional material that does not appear in the
ode, and now a leap over the ode's stanzas three through six. The
leap is significant; it creates an enormous discrepancy between
the antecedent of "The dark distressful Dream" in the *Letter* and
the antecedent of "Reality's dark dream" in the ode, from both of
which "I turn . . . and listen to the wind."

In the ode, "Reality's dark dream" is made up of the "viper
thoughts, that coil around my mind;" and these thoughts are
clearly meant to be the "abstruse research" of the preceding
stanza which he blames for his failure of imagination and feeling. But in the *Letter*, "The dark distressful Dream" is made up
of the pain he imaginatively inflicts on Sara. The alteration, in
the ode, is not complete, since the submerged animosity toward
and fear of Sara persists in the phrase "viper thoughts" which recalls the lamia in *Christabel*, the snakelike woman in his dream,
and all the phallic women whose presence afflicted him awake
and asleep.

Turning from the "dream"—an appropriate word choice—to
listen to the wind apparently does not work to relieve him, either
in the *Letter* or in the ode. Discomfort is apparent, for one thing,
in the number of cancellations that occur in the space of thirty-
one lines in the *Letter* in an unprecedented ratio for this mass of
verse which he apparently composed almost as fast as he could
write. There are four cancellations, in a piece that has run on for
as many as a hundred and twenty-one lines with only one cancellation:

> Nay, wherefore did I let it haunt my [*dr*] Mind
>   The dark distressful Dream!
> I turn from it, & listen to the Wind
> Which long has [*howl'd*] rav'd unnotic'd! What a Scream
> Of agony by Torture lengthen'd out

That Lute sent forth! O thou wild Storm without!
[*Steep Crag*] Jagg'd Rock, or mountain Pond, or Blasted
    Tree,
Or Pine-Grove, Whither Woodman never clomb,
Or lonely House, long held the Witches' Home,
Methinks were fitter Instruments for Thee,
Mad Lutanist! that in this month of Showers,
Of dark brown Gardens, & of peeping Flowers,
Mak'st Devil's Yule, with worse than wintry Song
The Blossoms, Buds, and timorous Leaves among!
Thou Actor, perfect in all tragic Sounds!
Thou mighty Poet, even to frenzy bold!
    What tell'st thou now about?
'Tis of the Rushing of an Host in Rout—
And many Groans from men with smarting Wounds—
At once they groan with smart, and shudder with the
    Cold!
Tis [sic] hush'd! there is a Trance of deepest Silence,
Again! but all that Sound [&] as of a rushing Crow'd [sic],
And Groans & tremulous Shudderings, all are over—
And it has other Sounds, and all less deep, less loud!
    A Tale of less Affright,
    And temper'd with Delight,
As William's Self had made the tender Lay
    'Tis of a little Child
    Upon a heathy Wild,
Not far from home—but it has lost it's way—
And now groans low in utter grief & fear—
And now screams loud, & hopes to make it's Mother hear!

Turning to the sound of the wind in an effort to escape bad
dreams proves to be simply a continuation of unpleasantness.
This section—of both the *Letter* and the ode—has to be read as
free association or it makes no sense whatever. Read this way, the
sense of it is that the hostile fantasies about Sara burst forth in a
crescendo of sado-masochistic feeling. The wind, which earlier in
the poem has appeared to be a destructive force, capable of still-

ing the lute, now has the power to torture it, both in the *Letter* and in the ode:

> I turn from it, and listen to the Wind
> Which long has [*howl'd*] rav'd unnotic'd! What a Scream
> Of agony by Torture lengthen'd out
> That Lute sent forth.

Judging from the use of the demonstrative *that* instead of *this* of stanza one, there seems to be an effort to locate the lute outside the self; but since the lute was clearly established in the beginning of the poem as a metaphor for the passive self, there is no reason to believe that this is anything more than an effort. It is the passive self that is being tortured by the wind, metaphor of something or someone in the external world; and the lute is set in contrast to various landscape details out of Gothic literature which the writer says "were fitter instruments for Thee,/ Mad Lutanist!"

Confusion sets in here, beginning with the apostrophe to the mad lutanist, which naturalistically ought to be the external wind but which in this context has all the attributes of the self that in the preceding stanza imagined pain and suffering for Sara. The effort to locate the lute outside the self is accompanied by a projection of unacceptable impulses onto the external wind. The mad lutanist certainly shares characteristics with the demon-lover of *Christabel*, as

> ... in this month of Showers,
> Of dark brown Gardens, & of peeping Flowers, [it]
> Mak'st Devil's Yule, with worse than wintry Song
> The Blossoms, Buds, and timorous Leaves among!

This wind, this mad lutanist, is satanic; and the flowers and leaves among which it "Mak'st Devil's Yule" suggest, as the landscape of *Kubla Khan* suggests, something besides agricultural fertility. The adjective *timorous* alone is enough to associate these growing things with the maiden in distress whose role Sara was made to perform in the stanza before.

But the confusing intertwining of subject and object in the passage precludes any one-to-one equivalence here; if the tortured lute is the passive self, it should be remembered that it is Sara who is the original, at least in this poem, of the heart within the heart—an identification that is made several lines later (line 250)—so that pain and suffering in this passage are being imagined for both Sara and the self, in a sado-masochistic mood that does double duty, as release of his aggressions toward Sara and as simultaneous self-punishment for these impulses.

More confusion is at work in the definition of the wind as

> ... Actor, perfect in all tragic Sounds!
> Thou mighty Poet, even to frenzy bold!

If the writer does not think of himself as a mighty poet, he does not think of himself at all; this is a clear case of a lack of distinction between inner and outer reality. The reference to the "Actor, perfect in all tragic Sounds," is an unconscious confession of his own life-long masquerade as a child of frailty whose tragic sounds had always been calculated to make him appear to be victim rather than victimizer.

A question follows, directed to the mighty poet: "What tell'st thou now about?" And the reply is reminiscent of *Christabel*, where Christabel and Geraldine pass through the gates "that were ironed within and without,/ Where an army in battle array had marched out."

> 'Tis of the Rushing of an Host in Rout—
> And many Groans from men with smarting Wounds—
> At once they groan with smart, and shudder with the Cold!

It is Coleridge himself who is telling about the suffering of soldiers; it becomes apparent that the mad lutanist, who tortures the lute with associations of this kind, is the unconscious, producing unacceptable and terrifying material: if the metaphor of lutanist and lute suggests satanic—rather than divine—inspiration, it ought to be pointed out that inspiration has always in literature

been simply a euphemism for the unconscious part of the personality, so that the confusion between subject and object which
dominates this part of the poem may be said to be the result of
the splitting of the self into victim and victimizer. No place in
Coleridge's poetry is he less in control of the warring parts of his
personality than he is here, where his fantasies of male assertion
and of female passivity explode into the imagined roles of victim
and victimizer, demon-lover and woman wailing for—and because of—him.

The mood was too intense to be sustained; the material, crowding into consciousness, had to be repressed, and repressed it is in
the next lines:

> Tis hush'd! there is a Trance of deepest Silence,
> Again! but all that Sound as of a rushing Crow'd,
> And Groans & tremulous Shudderings, all are over—
> And it has other Sounds, and all less deep, less loud!
>> A Tale of less Affright,
>> And temper'd with Delight,
> As William's Self had made the tender Lay
>> 'Tis of a little Child
>> Upon a heathy Wild,
> Not far from home—but it has lost it's way—
> And now groans low in utter grief & fear—
> And now screams loud, & hopes to make it's Mother hear!

The use of the conjunction *but* in the second line of this passage suggests that the impulse was to say that "all that Sound"
was *not* over, that it continued. If the logic of the passage were
to be sustained, the conjunction should have been *and* not *but*;
and so it is revised in the ode.[14] The need for the revision makes
it clear that the repression here is incomplete, an inference borne
out by the rest of the passage where the writer hears a "tale" that
expresses more overtly than any other detail in Coleridge's verse
his compulsion to repeat in literature one of the most emotionally charged events in his life: his runaway experience.

vii

With the repetition compulsion in mind, the decision to "listen to the Wind" takes on added implications. It becomes—like so many details in Coleridge's verse—an emotional gesture with conflicting motives. It has to be interpreted not only as an escape from bad dreams, but also, and paradoxically, as an effort to confront the material of those dreams in order to overcome it.

The wind appears to be Coleridge's unconscious; listening to it, he gives himself to the effort to collide with it and conquer it by the force of his shaping spirit, in the same way that he gave himself in childhood to the aggressively self-assertive act of running away when he found "a gloomy satisfaction" in making his mother "miserable," and in the same way that he gave himself to the effort of self-assertion by means of the "abstruse research" that led him to the formulation of a dynamic, independent concept of imagination. The collision produces, as his runaway experience and his metaphysical rebellion produced, violence, pain, and cold—the cold of man alone and on his own as a result of the usurpation of his father or his god. The confrontation of himself became the confrontation of his fantasies of male assertion; they were too painful to recognize; the confrontation was a failure.

In the ode, therefore, since both escape (repression) and confrontation had failed, Coleridge made certain changes which stiffened the mask of the child of frailty. The masculine pronouns of the *Letter* in the passage that recalls his runaway experience were changed to feminine pronouns. Again, the passive self was summoned to duty; the received text reads:

> 'Tis of a little child
> Upon a lonesome[15] wild,
> Not far from home, but she has lost her way:
> And now moans low in bitter[16] grief and fear,
> And now screams loud, and hopes to make her mother
>   hear.[17]

The failure of Coleridge's confrontation of his unconscious wishes brings him back, in the *Letter*, to the contrast between then and now which he had established in lines 44 through 51 of the *Letter*:

> My genial Spirits fail—
> And what can these avail
> To lift the smoth'ring Weight from off my Breast?
> It were a vain Endeavour,
> Tho' I should gaze for ever
> On that Green Light, which lingers in the West!
> I may not hope from outward Forms to win
> The Passion & the Life, whose Fountains are within!

He believed that then he could successfully control the disturbing unconscious material that fragmented his personality but that now he could not. Two means of control are indicated: literary elaboration and sexual release, which apparently existed for him simultaneously and interdependently.[18] Like all nostalgically imagined types of paradise lost, however, this one was illusory. The rhetoric of *Kubla Khan* would be enough to establish that for some years—at least—he had been the man who "cannot," even if it were not for the imperfect elaborations in *Osorio, Christabel*, and the *Rime*, and even if it were not for his grotesquely imperfect ability to relate to women. The effort to organize and control the conflicted parts of his personality had always been a "vain Endeavour" with regard both to his work and to his life.

It is notable that his failure in the face of his unconscious wishes leads him in the *Letter* directly to a statement about the failure of his poetic imagination. Following the stanza which became most of stanza seven in the ode are two stanzas which eventually contributed to the ode's eighth and again seventh stanzas:

> 'Tis Midnight! and small [*Hopes*] Thoughts have I of
> Sleep—
> Full seldom may my Friend such Vigils keep—

O breathe She softly in her gentle Sleep!
Cover her, gentle Sleep! with wings of Healing.
And be this Tempest but a mountain Birth!
May all the Stars hang bright about her Dwelling,
Silent, as tho' they *watch'd* the sleeping Earth!
Healthful & light, my Darling! may'st thou rise
    With clear & chearful Eyes—
And of the same good Tidings to me send!
    For, oh! beloved Friend!
I am not the buoyant Thing, I was of yore—
When like an own Child, I to *Joy* belong'd;[19]
For others mourning oft, myself oft sorely wrong'd,
Yet bearing all things then, as if I nothing bore!

    Yes, dearest Sara, yes!
There *was* a time when tho' my path was rough,
The Joy within me dallied with Distress;
And all Misfortunes were but as the Stuff
Whence Fancy made me Dreams of Happiness:
For Hope grew round me, like the climbing Vine,
And Leaves & Fruitage, not my own, seem'd mine!
But now [*Misfortunes*] Ill Tidings bow me down to earth/
Nor care I, that they rob me of my Mirth/
    But oh! each Visitation
Suspends what Nature gave me at my Birth,
My shaping Spirit of Imagination!
I speak not now of those habitual Ills
That wear out Life, when two unequal Minds
Meet in one House, & two discordant Wills—
    This leaves me, where it finds,
Past cure, & past Complaint—a fate Austere
Too fix'd & hopeless to partake of Fear!

The only genuine insight in these two stanzas is to be found at
the end of the second one, where he writes that his difficulty is
not to be accounted for by means of his unhappy marriage. There
is in the statement a large truth—that the trouble lies far deeper
and further in the past. And when he says that the marriage

leaves him "Past cure, & past Complaint," he is right. Objectively there was no reason for him not to leave his wife for Sara Hutchinson; and yet psychologically there was every reason for his inability to do so.

Except for this recognition, both stanzas are deceiving and deceived. The prayer for sleep for Sara—with the careful proviso that she should wake again—is an attempt to deny the submerged meaning of the preceding stanza; and its encirclement by self-pitying details does nothing to make it more persuasive. The afterthought about his past, "When like an own Child, I to *Joy* belong'd," is in powerful contrast to everything known about his childhood feelings. The concluding lines of the first stanza in this passage verge on paranoia in their detachment from the reality of his past life.

The second stanza's ambiguity suggests that, as usual, he is saying one thing and intending another. The crux of the unconscious irony is expressed in two lines:

> For Hope grew round me, like the climbing Vine,
> And Leaves & Fruitage, not my own, seem'd mine!

This vine looks like the water-snakes in the *Rime* and suggests the snakelike Geraldine and the snakelike woman in his dream; it is an image turned inside out. What "Hope" has he lost? What is suggested, and strongly, is the mother, the aboriginal phallic woman; if the maternal paradise of *Kubla Khan* is recalled here, the association is plain. The "Leaves & Fruitage" that were not his, but only seemed to be, suggest that he was deprived of the female sexual characteristics which he formerly imagined he had as a result of his identification through incorporation with his mother.[20] In at least two ways, then, he has lost the heart within the heart: first, in being deprived of his mother's full and exclusive and forbidden love; and second, in the failure of the identification to sustain itself, which means that he has also lost the possibility of intimacy with the father or with a father surrogate.

Both of these losses can be related to Sara Hutchinson: he believed he could not have her exclusive love (the Wordsworths, particularly William, stood between them); and of course he could not *be* her, notwithstanding his reference to her as the heart within the heart; nor could he maintain a relationship with her as a woman who was like a man.

Inextricable from this loss is another one:

> But oh! each Visitation
> Suspends what Nature gave me at my Birth,
> My shaping Spirit of Imagination!

What nature gave him at his birth was precisely his masculinity; and what he is feeling here is the effect of a succession of depressive states which seemed to him, because of his guilts, to be increasingly castrative. There is no conflict here with the notion of the "shaping Spirit of Imagination," since sexual power and creative power were for him simultaneous forms of assertive action.[21]

What all of this means is that he could not love or be loved by a woman or a man, nor could he behave fully and freely in the role of either sex. These failures go back to the first stanza of the *Letter* and the ode and repeat the despair that results from the unconscious wish to be androgynous[22] and the consequent inability to fulfill himself in either direction.

viii

The *Letter* continues, after the distinction between then and now, with an attempt to catalog the cures he had searched for in his discomfort and the pleasures that still remained for him. The attempt fills three stanzas, which do not appear in the ode, the first of which has a relatively large number of cancellations and one insertion, indicating emotional disturbance:

> But thou, dear Sara! (dear indeed thou art,
> My Comforter! A Heart within my Heart!)
> Thou, & the Few, we love, tho' few ye be,
> Make up a world of Hopes & Fears for me.

And [*when*] if Affliction, or distemp'ring Pain,
Or wayward Chance befall you, I complain
Not that I mourn—O Friends, most dear! most true!
　　Methinks to weep with you
Were better far than to rejoice alone—
But that my coarse domestic Life[23] has known
[*No mutual mild Enjoyments of it's own*]
No habits of heart-nursing Sympathy,
No Griefs but such as dull and deaden me,
[*No mutual mild Enjoyments of it's own*]
No Hopes of its own Vintage, None, o! none—
Whence when I mourn'd for you, my Heart might borrow
Fair forms & living Motions for it's Sorrow.
For not to think of what I needs must feel,
But to be still & patient all I can;
[*Or*] And haply by abstruse Research to steal
From my own Nature all the Natural Man—
This was my sole Resource, my wisest plan!
And that, which suits a part, infects the whole,
And now is almost grown the Temper of my Soul.

This stanza introduces overtly Coleridge's confusion about who it was who was his chief comfort and the object of his deepest feelings. Clearly it is not possible for him to choose Sara over her sister Mary and William and Dorothy Wordsworth, since it is

Thou, & the Few, we love, tho' few ye be, [*who*]
Make up a world of Hopes & Fears for me.

But he has said that "Hope [which] grew round me, like the climbing Vine," was gone; it can only be assumed that it is the submerged meaning of "hope" that persists for him in this world created by Sara and Mary and the Wordsworths, that it is the phallic qualities of "the Few" that continued to draw him, and in close association with "Fears." The world is made up of a man—a father surrogate—and three phallic women, all of whom represent to him the strongest possible danger.

The change in line five of the stanza just given from *when* to *if* is an attempt to deny his retaliatory wishes in the face of such danger; the cancelled *when* is the beginning of an expression of the wish that "Affliction, or distemp'ring Pain,/ Or wayward Chance [should] befall" these dangerous figures. Such an interpretation is strengthened by the succeeding lines in which he tries to rationalize what would be his inability to sympathize with his multiplied beloved in misfortune. He would complain, he says, not the ability to mourn but rather the inability to do so; and he fastens the blame for this hypothetical failure on his marriage, which has not accustomed him to "heart-nursing Sympathy." The lapse here from the earlier insight that told him his marriage was not the cause of his depression is critical; he is opportunistically contradicting himself. And that his feeling failure is not the result of his unhappy marriage—further, that the marriage is not entirely without "mild Enjoyments"—is made clear by the cancellation—twice—of the line "No mutual mild Enjoyments of it's own."

The familiar passage that begins "For not to think of what I needs must feel," both in the *Letter* and in the ode, which blames his "abstruse research" for his feeling failure, must be reinterpreted.[24] In the light of the tiny cancellation, from *Or* to *And*, it is clear that the "research" is an alternative to repression ("not to think of what I needs must feel") and is therefore not the cause of the feeling failure to the exclusion of his unconscious impulses but is only one more form of activity that stimulates these impulses.

The second stanza in the attempt to catalog comforts takes up the subject of his children:

> My little Children are a Joy, a Love,
>   A good Gift from above!
> But what is Bliss, that still calls up a Woe,
>   And makes it doubly keen
> Compelling me to *feel*, as well as KNOW,

What a most blessed Lot mine might have been.
Those little Angel Children (woe is me!)
There have been hours, when feeling how they bind
And pluck out the wing-feathers of my Mind,
Turning my Error to Necessity,
I have half-wish'd, they never had been born!
That seldom! But sad Thoughts they always bring,
And like the Poet's Philomel, I sing
My Love-song, with my breast against a Thorn.

Again reading his prayer book, he begins by acknowledging his children as a blessed gift from God. But then follows the confession, not surprising in view of the essentially infantile quality of his emotions, that he has sometimes "half-wish'd, they never had been born!" He goes on to italicize the infrequency of such wishes, in order to lessen them, but then doubles back to the declaration that "sad Thoughts they [the children] always bring."

There is of course an explanation for such wishes. Fixed as he was at an emotional level where his own needs were those of a child (a statistician might enjoy counting the occurrences of the word *child* as applied to himself in the letters, notebooks, and poems) making insatiable demands on both parents, his own children must have seemed like rivals to him. In addition, in April, 1802, he had only sons; Sara was not born until December of that year. Announcing her birth to Southey, Coleridge wrote:

I arrived at Keswick, with T. Wedgewood, on Friday afternoon—that is to say, yesterday—& had the comfort to find that Sara was safely brought to bed, the morning before—i.e. Thursday ½ past six, of a healthy—GIRL! I had never thought of a Girl as a possible event—the word[s][25] child & man child were perfect Synonimes in my feelings—[26]

When he wrote the *Letter*, therefore, on April 4, the idea of a daughter had not occurred to him. The history of his rivalrous relationships with his brothers—Frank in particular—as father surrogates, and of his ambivalent relationships with Southey, Poole, and Wordsworth, onto whom he displaced his feelings for his father when his brothers no longer could or would accede to his fantasies, has to be recollected in connection with this confession of death wishes for his sons, in whom it would have been impossible for him not to sense symbolically his brothers, and behind his brothers his father. Furthermore, his susceptibility to identification would have made him sense his sons symbolically as himself, in need of punishment.

Such symbolic substitution undoubtedly got reinforcement from the death of Coleridge's second son Berkeley in February, 1799, when he was less than a year old, and when Coleridge was in Germany on the journey he began with William and Dorothy Wordsworth in September 1798. The mood in which Coleridge acknowledged receipt of the news of his son's death was very much like the mood in which he acknowledged receipt of the news of Frank's death. He had been unable to feel "anguish" for Frank; about Berkeley he wrote to Poole (who sent him the news):

> ... I cannot truly say that I grieve—I am perplexed—
> I am sad—and a little thing, a very trifle would make
> me weep; but for the death of the Baby I have *not*
> wept![27]

This is hardly the ironic refusal to mourn made deliberately and in full awareness of its implications; it is the result of Coleridge's characteristic feeling failure when confronted by an event that startled his unconscious wishes and made them live. His failure to weep is expressed in the letter after a long, discursive passage of Christian idealism intended to prove immortality, so that apparently it was rationalized in advance. Following the statement that he has not wept for Berkeley, the letter continues:

> Oh! this strange, strange, strange Scene-shifter, Death!
> that giddies one with insecurity, & so unsubstantiates

the living Things that one has grasped and handled!—/
Some months ago Wordsworth transmitted to me a
most sublime epitaph/ whether it had any reality, I
cannot say.—Most probably, in some gloomier moment
he had fancied the moment in which his Sister might
die.

He transcribes the epitaph, which is "A Slumber Did My
Spirit Seal." Two months before Berkeley's death, Coleridge himself "in some gloomier moment . . . fancied the moment in which
his [son] might die." His wife wrote to him in November[28] that
Berkeley had recovered from the ill effects of a smallpox inocula-
tion, and in reply he wrote to her:

God, the Infinite, be praised that my Babes are alive.
His mercy will forgive me that late and all too slowly
I raised up my heart in thanksgiving.—At first and for a
time, I wept as passionately as if they had been dead—
and for the whole day the weight was heavy upon me,
relieved only by fits of weeping.—I had long expected,
I had passionately expected, a letter; I received it, and
my frame trembled—I saw your hand, and all feelings
of mind and body crowded together—had the news
been chearful & only, 'We are as you left us'—I must
have wept, to have delivered myself of the stress and
tumult of my animal sensibility—But when I read the
danger and the agony—My dear Sara!—my love! my
Wife!—God bless you & preserve us—I am well; but
a stye, or something of that kind, has come upon &
enormously swelled my eye-lids, so that it is painful
and improper for me to read or write![29]

Judging from the heat of this letter, which by the way is not
the only one in which he addressed passionate endearments to
his wife, in contrast to the coolness of the letter acknowledging
Berkeley's death, it seems clear that any emotionally significant
event was for him far more moving in fantasy than in reality:
Berkeley's death, like his love for Mary Evans, was a far more

powerful prospect than it was a reality. In any case, it is apparent from this letter that he did imagine the death of his sons, which is to say that he wished it. The guilt-inducing cluster of associations that must have surrounded the wish was strong enough, in fact, to produce in him a somatic disturbance of the eye.

Later on, after the actual death of Berkeley, he wrote to Poole that

> . . . I thought of my own verses on the Nightingale, only because I thought of Hartley, my *only* child!— Dear Lamb! I hope, *he* won't be dead, before I get home. —There are moments in which I have such a power of Life within me, such a conceit of it, I mean—that I lay the Blame of my Child's Death to my absence— *not intellectually*; but I have a strange sort of sensation, as if while I was present, none could die whom I intensely loved—and doubtless *it* was no absurd idea of your's that there may be unions & connections out of the visible world.[30]

Both the anxiety about Hartley and the superstition that his presence could forestall death are certainly symptoms of the kind of guilt that had led him in childhood to establish magical connections between his running away from home and his father's death and that led him later on to reestablish those magical connections in his suicidal enlistment in the army after Frank's death. It was these magical connections "out of the visible world" that obsessed him after Berkeley's death: Coleridge's trembling on the edge of psychoanalytic insight, as it shows itself for instance in the phrase he used in this letter, is frequently dazzling in its approach to the truth about himself. But it never helped him; he ended the letter to Poole:

> My dear Poole! don't let little Hartley die before I come home.—That's silly—true—& I burst into tears as I wrote it.

In the body of the letter to Poole in which he expresses his superstition, he recounts the story of a suicide in Germany, apparently only to entertain Poole with its strangeness; but the details of the story are so close to Coleridge's own internal and external situation that it is impossible not to see his fascination with it as an unconscious recognition of his own fantasies. Juxtaposed with his expression of guilt about Berkeley's death, this literal *liebestod* opens wide windows on the fantasies that inspired the guilt.

There have happened a multitude of Suicides in Germany within thes[e][31] last months; I have heard of eleven / and many of them curious enough. I relate the following, because I am sure of it's accuracy, & because it is quite *German*—i.e. it has quite a Schiller-ish, *Charles de Moorish Gloss* about it.—On the 3rd of Feb. Herlt, a Subaltern Officer in the Catholic Cours at Dresden, made a pleasure party in a Sledge with a woman whom he lived in criminal connection, called Wilhelmine Pfeifer. The[y] went to Heller, a little place in the midst of Woods two english miles from Dresden, to a Pleasure house there— / here they feasted most gloriously, & enjoyed themselves / & in conclusion, Herlt shot the Girl dead, & then himself.—He was a native of Bohemia, and had married a Tradesman's Daughter of Leibsic— but had lived unhappily with her, & become addicted to gambling & Drinking &c—he had long declared his intention of destroying himself, to which the impossibility of being divorced, it was supposed, had impelled him. This however is contradicted by himself in a letter directed to his wife, which was found after his death on the table in the place where he shot himself, acquainting her with his Intention. The following is an extract from this letter—'Forgive me—for ever!—In yonder World perhaps we see each other again. My Death was unavoidable—I and Thou are not the Causes; but

Wicked Men. . . . Death must have it's Causes; mine
has *it's*, has many causes which I will hold in silence.
It may be easily supposed, that the Prospect into Futurity
is a terrible one to me. But complain not. This Destiny
was appointed me by the same being who appointed
the Heavens & the Earth, and at the same time. . . .From
my Childhood Happiness has fled from me, [and]
Misfortune persecuted me, especially in my Marriage.
I utter no complaint against thee; for I knew that thou
wert a weak Woman! Now & hereby receiv'st [thou]/
intelligence of my Death. The woman, with whom I am,
I found by accident, loved her from day to day more
impetuously, and we are, as thou seest, inseparable. Our
Love cannot be legalized by Priests according to human
ordinances—in it's fitness to our being / it has legalized
itself. This is not the reason why I leave this world.
Thou knowest, how Mankind have treated me. . . . The
Death hour strikes—& we go! My Wilhelmine, last
Being to me, for us both there is but one Grave.—'
—At the bottom of this letter Wilhelmine wrote the
following, which in the original is in a wild irregular
Verse—'To die with Herlt is my Will, I hope with
exultation with thee, my Herlt! to die! And there
in yonder Glory with thee to take possession of our
Inheritance! I loved thee in life impetuously, in death
I love thee far more. Thou, whom I have found faithful,
come with me—let us go in triumph and ask Happiness
of the Being that made us. Beautiful was the hour, in
which thy fidelity was rewarded. (I presume, she means
the hour of her first seduction by Herlt.)[32]

There is more, but this abridged version will more than do.
The trouble Coleridge went to to translate and then to transcribe
this piece of Gothic real life certainly suggests that it served him
as a full if veiled confession to Poole of his paranoia and his sado-
masochistic fantasies. He follows it with some literary comments
about drama versus real life and then says he is homesick and to

prove it inserts the verses entitled "Homesick,"[33] which celebrate
the sabbath, marriage, children, home, and England. The death
of Berkeley had released full strength and in their accustomed
order his fantasies of aggression followed by the pose of the child
of frailty. The reason his children always stirred "sad Thoughts"
in him ought to be clear: Hartley and Derwent reminded him
that on three separate occasions a fearful wish of death for the
father, made for the purpose of having the exclusive love of the
mother, had been fearfully fulfilled.

His own need for punishment as a result of these disastrous
coincidences was constant. He concludes the stanza about the
children in the *Letter* with the observation that in loving them,

> ... like the Poet's Philomel, I sing
> My love-song, with my breast against a Thorn.

Philomel is a perfect choice for description of himself. A complete innocent in a narrative of violent sexuality, mutilation, and
metamorphosis, she is still the cause of all of it. Victim and victimizer meet again in the image of Philomel, as they met in
Christabel, to express precisely Coleridge's passive and aggressive impulses. The latent detail of mutilation is appropriate to his
fantasies of castration; the metamorphosis of Philomel into
nightingale corresponds to Coleridge's elaboration of his fantasies in poetry (song). And characteristically, he comes to rest in
this simile, as he did in *Christabel* and in the image of the "little
Child/ Upon a lonesome wild," in a female persona.

One more stanza in the *Letter* continues the flow of feeling
about his children, whom he finds, undoubtedly because of his
guilts, that he loves even more—though with less joy—because
of his "clinging Grief." From the children the stanza turns, as if
in duty bound, to scenes of nature as a possible consolation:

> I were sunk low indeed, did they *no* solace give;
> But oft I seem to feel, & evermore I fear,
> They are not to me now the Things, which once they were.

ix

The catalog in three stanzas having concluded disastrously, the
Letter presents three more stanzas in which the writer turns in
upon himself as the only source of consolation. The first of the
three concluding stanzas became stanza four of the ode, with only
two changes exclusive of punctuation. One change is important
—the significant shift from *Sara* in the *Letter* to *lady* in the ode.
The intervening changes—*William* and *Wordsworth* and *Edmund*—for this space should be recalled.[34]

> O Sara! we receive but what we give,
> And in *our* Life alone does Nature live.
> Our's is her wedding Garment, our's her Shroud—
> And would we aught behold of higher Worth
> Than that inanimate cold World allow'd
> To the poor loveless ever-anxious Crowd,
> Ah! from the Soul itself must issue forth
> A Light, a Glory, and a[35] luminous Cloud
>   Enveloping the Earth!
> And from the Soul itself must there be sent
> A sweet & potent Voice, of it's own Birth,
> Of all sweet Sounds the Life & Element.

Love and death return unmasked from the first stanza of the
Letter with its reference to the two moons; and their juxtaposition in a single line makes it clear—if it is not already clear—
that the writer was inhabiting a world exactly like the world of
Herlt and Wilhelmine, except that instead of acting out his fantasies he wrote them out, and his effort to impose that world on
Sara or any of the Wordsworths did not succeed as Herlt had
succeeded with Wilhelmine.

His refuge from the *liebestod* turns out to be himself, only
slightly less arrogantly detached from "the poor loveless ever-
anxious Crowd" than he had been in "Pain." The requirement
for receiving solace from nature turns out to be the ability to
create both the solace and nature itself; and since this ability is

expressed in diction that has connotations of sexuality, it has to be assumed that again he is equating creativity with sexuality. The metaphor establishes the wished-for situation of the persona as a male in a relationship with the female earth:

> Ah! from the Soul itself must issue forth
> A Light, a Glory, and a luminous Cloud
>> Enveloping the Earth!

What is necessary is that

> ... from the Soul itself must there be sent
> A sweet & potent Voice, of it's own Birth,
> Of all sweet Sounds the Life & Element.

It should be remembered that the *Letter* establishes at the outset an unconscious equivalence between sexuality and the word, so that this "Voice," described furthermore as "sweet & potent," has to be read as sexual power. The power suggests autoeroticism since it is "of it's own Birth," or at the very least the ability to be stimulated without stimuli. The sexual reference is strengthened in the last line by its definition as "Life & Element."

The *Letter*'s next, and penultimate, stanza became stanza five of the ode. It does little more than repeat and by this means re-emphasize the content of the stanza before it:

> O pure of Heart! thou need'st not ask of me
> What this strong music in the Soul may be,
>> What, & wherein it doth exist,
> This Light, this Glory, this fair luminous Mist,
> This beautiful & beauty-making Power!
> JOY, innocent Sara! Joy, that ne'er was given
> Save to the Pure, & in their purest Hour,
> JOY, Sara! is the Spirit & the Power,
> That wedding Nature to us gives in Dower
>> A new Earth and a new Heaven
> Undreamt of by the Sensual & the Proud!
> Joy is that strong Voice, Joy that luminous Cloud—
>> We, we ourselves rejoice!

And thence flows all that charms or ear or sight,
All melodies the Echoes of that Voice,
All Colors a Suffusion of that Light.

The "JOY . . ./ That wedding Nature to us gives in Dower"
recalls the ". . . shaping Spirit of Imagination" which was described as ". . . what Nature gave me at my Birth" in lines 241
and 242 of the *Letter*; and the connotations that attach to the
metaphor expressed earlier are strengthened in this metaphor by
the capitalized word *joy*. The synesthetic perception of swimming light in the first stanza is repeated here in "luminous Mist
. . . luminous Cloud" and in the use of a form of a cancelled word
in stanza one which here is attached to light: "a Suffusion of that
Light."[36] The connection of light—or power, as it plainly indicates—with liquid was made firm in the received version of the
ode by the insertion of a line following the observation that joy
is given only "to the Pure, & in their purest Hour." The inserted
line is "Life, and Life's effluence, cloud at once and shower."[37]
Not only does the line insist on its sexual connotation; it also re-
states the value, for Coleridge's desperate bisexual dilemma, of
autoeroticism: the joy is both container and contained.

That joy is given "only to the Pure, & in their purest Hour"
and that joy is what the writer feels he lacks can only mean that
he "cannot" because he is not pure; and the way in which he is
not pure is the result of his forbidden knowledge, his experience
of and imagined participation in the primal scene of love between the parents, which created his latent bisexuality, the conviction of sin, and the paralytic dilemma.

The rhetoric of rivalry that dominates *Kubla Khan* sets in
very strongly here in the distinction between the writer and the
person he addresses: Sara, or William or Mary or Dorothy—or
Poole—"can," because they have presumably not acquired such
forbidden knowledge, while the writer "cannot" because he has.
This adds some ambiguity to the stanzas in the *Letter* that lament
the feeling failure in the fantasy that Sara (or whoever) sees the

same sky, with its omen of death (the primal scene), that the writer sees. Part of the failure must be the preconscious intuition that the person he addresses does in fact not see what he sees, that he is not addressing a Wilhelmine.

The concluding stanza of the *Letter* contributed only a couple of lines—and those with alterations—to the concluding, or eighth, stanza of the ode. As it stands in the *Letter* it has, in the space of seventeen lines, the insertion of two lines and a word, and two cancellations. The changes occur in the last six lines, which means that he had some difficulty in concluding the letter. This final stanza is on the surface an extravagant eulogy of Sara Hutchinson and a blessing for her:

> Sister & Friend of my devoutest Choice!
> Thou being innocent & full of love,
> And nested with the Darlings of thy Love,
> And feeling in thy Soul, Heart, Lips, & Arms
> Even what the conjugal & mother Dove,
> That borrows genial Warmth from those, she warms,
>   Feels in thrill'd wings, blessedly outspread—
> Thou free'd awhile from Cares & human Dread
> By the Immenseness of the Good & Fair,
>   Which thou seest every where—
> Thus, thus, should'st thou rejoice!
> To thee would all Things live from Pole to Pole,
> Their Life the eddying of thy living Soul.[38]
> O dear! O Innocent! O full of Love!
> [*A gentle*] A very Friend![39] A Sister[s] of my Choice—
> O dear, as Light & Impulse from above,
> Thus may'st thou ever, evermore rejoice!

But what the stanza actually does is to set Sara firmly in the warm nest of the Wordsworths; and the picture is too vivid a representation of happiness in contrast with the self-pitying view of himself that is presented in the *Letter* not to be the result of envy and the animosity that accompanies it. The writer sees her, furthermore, as a mother, and as a mother dove at that, which

not only recalls Christabel's dove-like aspect—clearly one side of
her nature only—and therefore makes the image and the expression suspect, but it suggests also Coleridge's identification with
his mother, the lapse of which was seen earlier in the *Letter* to
have caused him pain. He is establishing Sara here as the "good"
wife and mother ("the conjugal and mother Dove"), forever unattainable, forever tabu, and in his fantasies the woman he not
only cannot love or be loved by but also the woman he cannot
be.

He wishes for her the sky without the death omen:

> To thee would all Things live from Pole to Pole,
> Their Life the Eddying of thy living Soul,

but the wish is an afterthought that had to be inserted between
the lines already composed; it is the result of effort. And the cancellations in line 338 reveal respectively the pressure of his unconscious animosity and the effort to restrict his field of vision to
the single woman he is ostensibly writing to: "A gentle Friend"
he could not bring himself to write, hostile and envious as he
was toward this phallic woman; and his multiple beloved came
crowding his consciousness so that he had to insert the article
(indefinite, to be sure) *A* and cancel the plural *s* he unthinkingly
added to *Sister* in a final effort to single out Sara from "those, I
love, as I love thee,/ Mary, & William, & dear Dorothy."

8. Conclusion

Between each one of these Lines another might have been written with ease & perfect Legibility, I am extravagant. This Pocket book cost 9ˢ, 6ᵈ.—Coleridge

Without going into detail once more about the various revisions of the salutations in the *Letter* that were made between its composition and its final revision for *Sibylline Leaves*, it has to be recalled at this point that in several letters Coleridge presented versions and quotations from this flood of love and hate, envy and fear, with the salutations *William* and *Wordsworth* and *Poet*. The whole mass of verse, therefore, has to be read and interpreted at least twice—and a third time in the *Sibylline Leaves* version that is the received text of the ode.

The second reading has to account for Coleridge's motivation in addressing this renunciatory farewell, with all its connotations of sexual love, to William Wordsworth. The evidence argues that he felt about Wordsworth precisely as he felt about Sara Hutchinson. In making the *Letter* serve a dual purpose—as a farewell to Sara and as a farewell to Wordsworth—he demonstrated conclusively his compulsion to repeat not only the aggressions that underlay his runaway experience and the fears that stimulated his dreams but also his experience of the primal scene. Writing first to Sara and then to Wordsworth he was reenacting that experience fully, first in the role of the father and then in the role of the mother. This is not to suggest that the two roles were ever clearly separated for him; whether the salutation is *Sara* or *William*, the verse-writing represented to him the per-

165

formance of a double role, since he had a powerful need for a woman who was like a man and simultaneously for a man who was like a woman.

The third reading has to account for the massive shifts in organization that took place when he made the revisions for the *Morning Post* and the further revisions that he made for *Sibylline Leaves*, as well as for the deletion of great chunks of material. The deletion is relatively easy to account for. He removed mainly the most threatening material: the parallels with *Christabel* and the *Rime* and the reference to "dear William's Sky Canoe" which are irrelevant except to his fantasies; and a hundred and thirty-one lines of badly disguised hostile aggressiveness, also irrelevant to the poem.

That the deletions accomplished only a partial disguise of Coleridge's emotions seems pretty clear, since the ode as it stands in its final version retains fully the essence of his violently ambivalent feelings. In the *Morning Post* version which disguises *William* by means of *Edmund*, presumably in an effort not to air his autobiography, the feelings are plain. The return full-circle to *lady* in *Sibylline Leaves*, on the other hand, appears to be an unconscious impulse to deny his unconscious homoerotic attachment to Wordsworth, accompanied perhaps by increased animosity toward Wordsworth and an attendant refusal to recognize him even in the use of the masculine gender.

The shifts in organization appear to have been made partly for reasons of coherence but also partly in order to suppress as far as possible the real reasons for his depression. It was undoubtedly far easier for him to assign the cause of the depression to metaphysical speculation than it would have been to let the poem stand as a revelation of the sado-masochistic fantasies that paralyzed his feeling and his behavior. He did as much as he could to prevent such revelation but in spite of his efforts enough of a residue exists in the ode to send any reader who is interested in psychodynamics back to the primitive form of the poem. The

Dejection ode depends for its life as a piece of literature on the feelings that are floating free in the *Letter* and that in the ode itself are tightly compressed and refined to their essence.

Footnotes

Chapter One

[1] The few exceptions are significant. They appear to represent a healthy trend, away from the dogma of *l'art pour l'art* of the old New Critics, and toward the even older—and inescapable—definition of art as a thing made by someone in some place and at some time. What begins to look like neo-Freudianism in criticism performs best when it applies the lessons in close reading learned from the fallacy-founding fathers who twenty years ago would have made it indiscreet for men like Edward E. Bostetter and Douglas Angus to write as they have on Coleridge, or for F. W. Bateson to re-interpret Wordsworth. Since this was written, Geoffrey Yarlott has brought out his *Coleridge and the Abyssinian Maid* (London, 1967). I regret exceedingly that it is too late to consider his arguments in detail, especially since he is the only other writer who has attempted to explicate *A Letter to ——*. He has also referred to some of the correspondence and notebook entries for the purpose of defining the nature of Coleridge's dejection—in short, he has covered some of the same ground that underlies the progress of this book. The rather acute disagreements between us can perhaps be accounted for by differences in method: we read the terrain through different field glasses.

[2] Marshall Suther, *The Dark Night of Samuel Taylor Coleridge* (New York, 1960), 64.

[3] *Ibid.*, 66. Suther is far from uninterested in psychoanalytic method. He relies heavily in this book on a Freudian study by David Beres (see *infra*, 85 n.3), and in his more recent *Visions of Xanadu* (New York, 1965) it is clear, from his references to other psychoanalytic writers as well as from some of his interpretations, that he is not entirely free of Freudian (and sometimes Jungian) habits of mind.

Chapter Two

[1] Ernest de Selincourt, "Coleridge's *Dejection: an Ode*," *Essays and Stud-*

ies by Members of the English Association (1937), XXII (hereinafter noted as DES), 7-26. Reprinted in his *Wordsworthian and Other Studies* (Oxford, 1947). See also *Collected Letters of Samuel Taylor Coleridge*, ed. Earl Leslie Griggs (Oxford, 1956), (hereinafter noted as CL), II, 790.

[2] CL, II, 796.

[3] *Ibid.*, II, 796.

[4] *Ibid.*, II, 794.

[5] *The Journals of Dorothy Wordsworth*, ed. Ernest de Selincourt (London, 1952), (hereinafter noted as DWJ), I, 135-6.

[6] *Loc. cit.* The imagery of lambs and primroses is to be found also in Wordsworth's *Intimations* ode. Dorothy's reference to "the well, which we cleaned out last night," suggests the "stifled, drowsy, unimpassioned grief,/ Which finds no natural outlet," in the second stanza of the received version of the *Dejection* ode, since the well appears to be stagnant—"it is still but a muddy little pond"—and since it is "full of water." Her reference to the well seems to be an unconscious response to the unconscious implication of psychic impotence in the *Dejection* image.

[7] CL, II, 801.

[8] *Ibid.*, II, 814 ff.

[9] DES, *passim.* See also CL, II, 971-2.

[10] *The Complete Poetical Works of Samuel Taylor Coleridge*, ed. Ernest Hartley Coleridge (Oxford, 1957), (hereinafter noted as PWC), II, 1077-80.

[11] CL, I, 57.

[12] *Ibid.*, I, 63, 67.

[13] *Ibid.*, I, 80.

[14] *Ibid.*, I, 9-10.

[15] *Cf.* discussion of *Kubla Khan, infra,* 91-100. The emotional value of explosive imagery, for Coleridge, is especially emphasized, *infra,* 95 and n.24.

[16] CL, I, 53.

[17] Lawrence Hanson, *The Life of Samuel Taylor Coleridge* (New York, 1962), (hereinafter noted as HL), 33.

[18] CL, I, 5.

[19] *Ibid.*, I, 61-2. Griggs's headnote to Coleridge's letter to G. L. Tuckett.

[20] There seems no reason to doubt Griggs's assertion, in the headnote referred to in note 19, *supra*, that "the young men at Christ's Hospital" informed Tuckett of Coleridge's whereabouts and that Tuckett then so informed George.

[21] Hanson uses the term "self-abasement" and attributes to Coleridge "a readiness, not to say a genius" for it. See HL, 37.

[22] CL, I, 63-4.

[23] *Ibid.,* I, 82.

[24] Vera Watson, "Coleridge's Army Service," *Times Literary Supplement* July 7, 1950, 428. Earl Leslie Griggs, "Coleridge's Army Experience," *English,* IX (1953), 171-75. See also CL, I, 76.

[25] CL, I, 123. See also *ibid.,* I, 118: "I have heard from my Brothers— from him particularly, who has been friend, Brother, Father—'Twas all remonstrance, and Anguish, & suggestions, that I am deranged!!"

[26] *Ibid.,* I, 133.

[27] *Ibid.,* I, 105.

[28] *Ibid.,* I, 132.

[29] Coleridge was apparently an unreliable Greek scholar. According to Carl Roebuck of the Classics Department at Northwestern University, this phrase is syntactically illogical, and its other defects have not been wholly corrected by Griggs, although his bracketed ὑφορᾷς is precise enough. Καυχάω should properly be put in the middle voice as Καυχάομαι and should be followed by a full stop or a semi-colon. Roughly, the translation is "I boast of my life even though you view me with suspicion."

[30] CL, I, 149.

[31] *Ibid.,* I, *passim.*

[32] *Ibid.,* I, 150.

[33] *Ibid.,* I, 163-73.

[34] The coolness between Coleridge and Southey apparently began during the summer of 1795. See E. K. Chambers, *Samuel Taylor Coleridge* (Oxford, 1950), (hereinafter noted as ChL), 41-44. See also CL, I, *passim.*

[35] ChL, 45.

[36] CL, I, 168.

[37] *Ibid.,* I, 171.

[38] *Loc. cit.*

[39] *Ibid.*, I, 173.

[40] *Ibid.*, I, 302.

[41] *Ibid.*, I, 347. See also Douglas Angus, "The Theme of Love and Guilt in Coleridge's Three Major Poems," *Journal of English and Germanic Philology*, LIX (Oct., 1960), 655-668, for an interesting and valuable sketch of some of the unconsciously produced symbolism in *Osorio, Christabel, Kubla Khan*, and the *Rime*. Angus refers to some of the autobiographical material in the letters to Poole, in an effort to account for Coleridge's psychic discomforts. His reading of the poems is extremely interesting, but I cannot agree with his conclusion that

> With the writing of "Kubla Khan" this brief and glorious period of intensely imaginative creation by Coleridge came to an abrupt end. Never again would he open that dark window, although he tried most desperately to finish "Christabel." "I tried & tried," he writes, "& nothing would come of it. I desisted with a deeper dejection than I am willing to remember" (*Letters*, I, 643).

Coleridge's reference to "dejection"—in fact to "a deeper dejection than I am willing to remember"—suggests a connection, between the great dejection ode and the "emotion-laden symbols," that appears to contradict Angus's notion of the "brief" if "glorious period of intensely imaginative creation." The Coleridge canon is of course not steadily glorious, but if it has a high point of "intensely imaginative creation," that point occurs well after *Kubla Khan*, in *Dejection*. The "emotion-laden symbols" that contribute to the peculiar energy of Coleridge's verse, however, do not appear and disappear at fixed intervals; although their references shift and develop, they remain constant throughout the progress of his poetry-making and do a good deal to unify even his apparently fragmentary and disconnected works.

[42] CL, I, 352.

[43] *Ibid.*, I, 352-53.

[44] *Ibid.*, I, 353.

[45] *Loc. cit.*

[46] *Ibid.*, I, 353-54.

[47] *Ibid.*, I, 354.

[48] *Ibid.*, I, 347.

[49] ChL, 5.

[50] CL, 123.

[51] In his letters to Southey he was frequently at pains to deny his feelings of anger. See especially CL, I, 105, 102.

[52] CL, I, 354.

[53] *Ibid.*, I, 355.

[54] James Gillman, *The Life of Samuel Taylor Coleridge* (London, 1838), (hereinafter noted as GL), 10-11.

[55] CL, I, 311.

[56] *Ibid.*, I, 348.

[57] *Ibid.*, I, 311.

[58] *Ibid.*, I, 53.

[59] *Loc. cit.*

[60] GL, 50-51. ChL, 19. HL, 31. CL, I, 47.

[61] ChL, 19.

[62] CL, I, 55.

[63] See *infra*, Chapter III, for his mistakes about the ages of his brother Luke and his sister Anne. He is frequently wrong when he gives his age relative to others', *i.e.*, CL, I, 47: "I am just two months older than he [Samuel Butler, who won the Craven schoalrship in Cambridge in competition with Coleridge, apparently because under its terms the prize was to be awarded to the youngest competitor] is." Griggs notes that "Coleridge was 15 months Butler's senior." He notes also (CL, I, 118) that Coleridge all his life referred to his birthday as the 20th of October. He was born October 21, 1772. His other modifications of the facts of time will be pointed out as they are relevant.

[64] GL, 43.

[65] *Ibid.*, 49.

[66] *Ibid.*, 56, n.

[67] *Ibid.*, 56.

[68] *Ibid.*, 41-2. ChL, 21. HL, 30. CL, I, 68-9, 75, headnote. There is a suggestion, however, that even the debts were not so realistically pressing as Coleridge and his biographers would have us believe. Gillman, commenting that "Debt was to him at all times a thing he most dreaded" and that "he never had the courage to face it," repeats a story that "these College debts were about *one hundred pounds*! Under a hundred pounds I believe to have been the amount of his sinnings; but report exceeded this

(GL, 42)." Of course Gillman's source for this information was, as he writes, "thirty years afterwards"; but it is probably safe to assume that Coleridge over-reacted to his financial obligations as he did to other events of this period.

[69] CL, I, 59.

[70] *Loc. cit.*

[71] *Ibid.*, I, 61. PWC, I, 54-5.

[72] PWC, I, 54.

[73] Gillman finds the cause in "inward grief" brought about by Middleton's departure and the debts (GL, 56). Chambers recognizes a suicidal mood but offers counter evidence in Christopher Wordsworth's account of Coleridge's participation in jolly festivities in Cambridge during the week before his second exit from Cambridge and his enlistment in the army; he attributes Coleridge's depression, however, to the fact that "his pecuniary troubles were complicated by a 'love-fit.' Evidently his sentimental affair with Mary Evans had at last flamed into something like a passion. Probably he had seen her in London during October and had come to fear the existence of a rival. [See Chapter III, *infra*, for the suggestion that the "rival" was not feared but welcomed.] His own fortunes did not permit him to make a declaration" (ChL, 22). Hanson finds that he enlisted because he was "without money, incapable of forming plans, afraid to go back to Cambridge [because of the debts], and ashamed to remain in London where a meeting with the Evanses was difficult to avoid" (HL, 35). Griggs asserts that "His love for Mary Evans may have been a contributing cause of his enlistment . . . but it was his college debts which precipitated his action (CL, I, 61)."

[74] CL, I, 66-7.

[75] CL, I, 68.

[76] *Ibid.*, I, 63-4. *Cf.* Coleridge's letter to Tuckett on the preceding day (*ibid.*, I, 62): "The anguish of those who love me—of him [George], beneath the shade of whose protection I grew up—does it not plant my pillow with thorns, and make my dreams full of terrors? . . . Alas! my poor Mother!"

[77] *Ibid.*, I, 68.

[78] GL, 11-12n.

[79] *Cf.* PWC, I, 174, lines 18-19.

Chapter Three

[1] The verb *to elaborate* denotes the amplification of unconscious material. In literature the process reproduces, with amplification and distortion, unconscious experience of the writer.

[2] The dynamics of exhibitionism includes the compulsion to see what is hidden or forbidden; the wish to expose the self is a disguised signal of the wish to see the other. The object of voyeurism, no matter how it is disguised, is basically the primal scene of love between the parents. Fragments of the scene, or glimpses of hidden physical features of one of the parents or a parent surrogate (substitute) may serve as objects.

[3] CL, I, 304.

[4] The hysteria with which Coleridge doubted Poole's wish to have him as a neighbor was part of the tension that preceded Coleridge's eventual choice of Wordsworth over Poole as his father surrogate. See CL, I, 269-276, *passim*.

[5] CL, I, 352.

[6] *Loc. cit.* See also *ibid.*, I, 355-56.

[7] The imagery of the *Rime*, for example, turns up in a dream in 1802, the night before the publication of the *Dejection* ode. The relation between Coleridge's verse writing and his dreams is of substantial importance and is treated in later chapters.

[8] See *supra*, 21-29. Arnold B. Fox, in "The Biographical Background of Coleridge's *Osorio*," *Journal of English and Germanic Philology*, LXI (1962), 258-267, suggests George Coleridge as the object of ambivalent feelings which Coleridge expressed by means of resemblances to him in the characters of both Albert and Osorio; but Angus's article (see *supra*, 171, n.41) is more to the point. Angus presents evidence for Coleridge's oedipal problems and suggests that *Osorio* expresses the old rivalry with Frank and "the hidden murder of a father image [Ferdinand]," although strangely enough Angus says the murder is "without motivation" and also believes that Osorio plans to kill Albert himself and then decides to kill Ferdinand instead. The narrative does not support either notion.

[9] PWC, II, 522, lines 97-8.

[10] *Ibid.*, II, 539, lines 102-3.

[11] The title of the revised work is *Remorse*. See PW, II, 812 ff.

[12] PWC, II, 1114.

[13] *The Poetical Works of Wordsworth*, ed. Ernest de Selincourt (London, 1956), 38, line 664.

[14] *Op. cit.* See also Edward E. Bostetter, *The Romantic Ventriloquists* (Seattle, 1963), 82-135. See Yarlott, *op. cit.*, for a different view of the matter.

[15] Suther, *op. cit.*, 32-3.

[16] PWC, I, 78-9.

[17] Suther, *op. cit.*, 33.

[18] PWC, I, 21.

[19] *Ibid.*, I, 20. Cf. the reference to death's "icy dart" with his father's dream (*supra*, 24). The old associations are working here.

[20] CL, I, 311.

[21] *Loc. cit.*

[22] The nympholeptic quest, based as it is on psychic inversion that proceeds from incomplete sexual identification, disguises its real homoerotic aim by means of a neo-platonic dichotomy between the real and the ideal; the essential quality of this quest is that it is never fulfilled in what the poet calls real life, but can find an object only in what he calls the ideal world. See in this connection the concluding lines of "Happiness" (PWC, I, 30-32):

> Ah! doubly blest, if Love supply
> His influence to complete thy joy,
> If chance some lovely maid thou find
> To read thy visage in thy mind.

What Coleridge wants here is a woman who will love him not for his real self, which would have to include his physical appearance, but for his ideal self, for the essence he imagines himself to have. The denial of reality here is quite as strong as it is in Shelley's "Epipsychidion."

[23] CL, I, 354.

[24] *The Notebooks of Samuel Taylor Coleridge*, ed. Kathleen Coburn (New York, 1957), (hereinafter noted as CN), I, 750 5-½.6.

[25] *Loc. cit.*, n.

[26] CL, I, 354.

[27] CN, I, 263 G. 260.

[28] *Ibid.*, I, 264 G.261. The suggestion here is that the mother is some sort of goddess. See J. Garth Ware, "Coleridge's Great Poems Reflecting the Mother Image," *American Imago*, XVIII (1961), 331-352.

[29] The term *liebestod* is borrowed from the opera, *Tristan und Isolde,* by Richard Wagner, where it is used to denote the death of the two lovers at the peak of their love for each other and in the face of insurmountable obstacles to their love. Wagner's dramatization of the forbidden nature of courtly love and of its resolution in death is the most spectacular example in art of the expression of guilt in the presence of tabu. See Chapter VII *infra* for a fuller discussion of Coleridge's preoccupation with the *liebestod* theme.

[30] See Chapter V *infra.*

[31] Luke was seven years older than Samuel, only a year younger than George. He died in 1790 at the age of 25. While Samuel was a schoolboy in London, Luke was apparently beginning his medical career there and inspired his younger brother to an intense if temporary devotion to the paraphernalia of surgery. *Cf. supra,* Chapter II, for associations among Coleridge's brother Frank, the father, and the knife. It appears that Samuel's endowment of George with the paternal role was an attempt to replace Frank, who was his next eldest brother, and that if Luke had lived he might have spared George the pain of being regarded as the father surrogate.

[32] This is sister Anne who died in 1791. The archness and artificiality of the compliment suggest distance between Anne and Samuel. Like Mary Evans she was not "real" to him.

[33] These are Coleridge's father's daughters by his first wife Mary Lendon.

[34] CL, I, 1.

[35] *Loc. cit.,* n.: "Coleridge probably refers to James Burgh, *The Art of Speaking,* 1761."

[36] James Dykes Campbell, *Samuel Taylor Coleridge* (London, 1896), 6.

[37] *Specimens of the Table Talk of the late S.T.C.,* ed. H. N. Coleridge (London, 1851), (hereinafter noted as TT), 196.

[38] PWC, I, 20.

[39] The evidence is Coleridge's word for it, which is usually unreliable about chronology. But the dream he recorded on October 4, 1802, which is discussed *infra,* Chapter IV, suggests that even if he was wrong about the date of composition of these verses he nevertheless associated the constellation of feelings expressed in it with the nurse's daughter.

[40] PWC, I, 17.

[41] *Loc. cit.*

[42] *Ibid.*, I, 19 n.

[43] HL, 22.

[44] CL, I, 21-2.

[45] *Ibid.*, I, 22.

[46] *Loc. cit.*

[47] CL, I, 48. Coleridge's benevolism had its limits. In January of 1797 he sent Poole an invitation to dinner, in verse, with this postscript:

> Besides, we've got some cabbage—
> You Jew-dog, if you linger
> May the Itch in pomp of Scabbage
> Pop out between each finger (CL, I, 296).

The verse invitation is reprinted in PWC, II, 978, complete, but its first publication, in *Thomas Poole and his Friends* (London, 1881), I, 211, omitted the postscript. It makes an odd companion piece to the lines "To a Young Ass" (PWC, I, 74-5), a bathetic expression of benevolism. Weighing the animal and the Jew in the scale of Pantisocracy raises the question whether the whole Pantisocratic scheme were not an ornate disguise for his hostilities. The scheme of course never came to anything.

[48] CL, I, 49. *Cf.* Dorothy Wordsworth's reference to the well (Chapter II, 7-8 and n.6). Coleridge's psychic impotence is demonstrated fully in his relationship with Mary Evans.

[49] See Angus, *op. cit.*, who refers (656) to "his odd courtship of Mary Evans, in which he seems to have spent more time at the knee of the girl's mother than with the girl."

[50] CL, I, 88.

[51] ChL, 22.

[52] See n.48, *supra.*

[53] *Loc. cit.*

[54] CL, I, 88.

[55] CL, I, 109-10.

[56] *Ibid.*, I, 112-13.

[57] *Ibid.*, I, 113 n.

[58] A young lady who came to London with a theatrical company.

[59] CL, I, 113.

[60] *Ibid.*, I, 107 n.

[61] *Ibid.*, I, 121.

[62] Fryer Todd. He and Mary Evans were married October 13, 1795.

[63] CL, I, 130.

[64] *Ibid.*, I, 144.

[65] *Loc. cit.*

[66] *Ibid.*, I, 145.

[67] *Loc. cit.*

[68] *Loc. cit.*

[69] *Loc. cit.*

[70] Carl Woodring, in his *Politics in the Poetry of Coleridge* (Madison, 1961), discusses Alhadra as an "oppressed" infidel but grants that she is "fierce," and finds that "Genuine passion against tyrannical injustice, not trumped up to satisfy Sheridan, helped make Alhadra the strongest figure in the play. Several long speeches contain vignettes of pathos, Coleridgian in melancholia. . . . Yet Alhadra is frequently onstage to demonstrate successfully, as well as to proclaim, that 'Great evils ask great passions to redress them.'" Woodring goes on to say that "the public theme of victory of the persecuted meek over the tyrannically powerful stands in *Osorio* close behind the personal theme of remorse: The only worthy power is power over the self (*Op. cit.*, 204)." What Woodring refers to as Coleridge's "passion against tyrannical injustice" could not possibly have been, as he says, "genuine" except when he fancied himself its victim or, more important, when he felt that he deserved punishment. For a suggestion that his benevolism was less than pure, see *supra*, n.47. It is not "genuine passion against tyrannical injustice" that "helped make Alhadra the strongest figure in the play," but rather his powerful need for punishment at the hands of just such a powerful figure. Making her an oppressed infidel was a means of disguise—like the scheme of Pantisocracy—for his hostilities, and it was also a means of indicating that since she was "inferior," Osorio's death at her hands was not "really" Coleridge's own death.

[71] CL, I, 145.

Chapter Four

[1] *Christabel* and *Kubla Khan* were first published in 1816, together with *The Pains of Sleep*. In his preface to *Christabel*, Coleridge gives 1797 as the date of composition of the first part and 1800 as the date of composition of the second part (PWC, I, 213). The date of composition of

Kubla Khan, according to Coleridge's statement (PWC, I, 295), was 1797. The dating of both poems, however, is still a vexed question.

² The only writers who understand that Coleridge's feelings for Sara Hutchinson were not what he believed them to be are Marshall Suther in *The Dark Night of Samuel Taylor Coleridge* and Edward E. Bostetter in *The Romantic Ventriloquists*. Bostetter's work is one of the best treatments of the relationship between Coleridge's conscious and unconscious experiences.

³ The October notebook entries usually express disturbance. See particularly CN, I, 832 4.113 and n. and 833 21.74 n. for comparison between feelings expressed on his birthday in 1800 and the imagery of the *Dejection* ode.

⁴ Coburn associates this detail to his runaway experience (CN, I, 1250 21.214 n.).

⁵ Coburn considers *smokelike* a doubtful reading and presents *snakelike* in brackets. See CN, I, 1250 21.214 n. *Snakelike* is certainly a likely attribute of the "frightful pale woman" in view of the associations to her that are revealed in a careful study of the dream, although of course smoke could appear to be serpentine.

⁶ CN, I, 1250 21.214.

⁷ See again CN, I, 1250 21.214 n.

⁸ *Loc. cit.*

⁹ *The Works of Charles and Mary Lamb*, ed. Edward Verrall Lucas (London, 1903-05), II, 13. See ChL, 8: "For Lamb's 'Calne' we must of course read Ottery."

¹⁰ *Cf.* the detail of "nurse's daughters" with "Pain" and "Genevieve" which he associated with the actual nurse's daughter. See *supra*, 47 and n.

¹¹ An argument has been advanced that the phrase, "three persons and one soul," frequently attributed to Coleridge as a description of his relationship with William and Dorothy Wordsworth, is the result of mistranslation into German and subsequent translation back into English and that the original phrase suggests "an earlier date than is generally accepted for the cooling of Coleridge's hero-worship." See Ruth I. Aldrich, "The Wordsworths and Coleridge: 'Three Persons' But *Not* 'One Soul,'" *Studies in Romanticism*, II (1962), 61-3. Examination of the original phrase in its context, however, does not support the argument. The context is a letter to Godwin from London, which complains of "A

great change from the society of W. & his sister—for tho' we were three persons, it was but one God—" (CL, II, 775).

[12] See Bostetter, 131: "Coleridge's biography furnishes ample evidence of the way in which from childhood he made those who loved him and those upon whom he was dependent suffer."

[13] *Memoir and Letters of Sara Coleridge*, ed. Edith Coleridge (London, 1873), I, 19-20.

[14] *Cf.* Sara's "fair skin."

[15] *Cf.* Coleridge's life-long respiratory ailments.

[16] See Chapter III for discussion of this shift, in his fantasies as well as in *Osorio*.

[17] *Loc. cit.*

[18] Both these meanings were in use at the time Coleridge wrote. See the *New Oxford English Dictionary*.

[19] See N.E.D.

[20] *Supra*, 6 and n.

[21] See Angus, *op. cit.*, 659, for the suggestion that Coleridge's ambivalence toward his mother produces the battles between "good" and "bad" spirits in the *Rime* and *Christabel*.

[22] PWC, I, 226, lines 298-301.

[23] At the moment, his "love" would be Mary Evans.

[24] PWC, I, 234, lines 616-20.

[25] *Ibid.*, lines 643-46.

[26] Schulz discusses *Christabel* as a poem written in the "ventriloquism voice" (61), without reference to a mask, conscious or unconscious. Bostetter finds that Coleridge "links himself with both Geraldine and Christabel" (130); he refers to Freud's theory of the repetition compulsion and finds it operative in *Christabel* (127); he recognizes sadistic elements in the poem (131); and he is the only writer besides Yarlott (*op. cit.*) who refers to Coleridge's dreams (120). Angus sees "an identification of the poet with Christabel (663)."

[27] PWC, I, 216, lines 6-13.

[28] *Ibid.*, I, 223, lines 204-13.

[29] Roy P. Basler, in *Sex, Symbolism, and Psychology* (New Brunswick, 1948), observes "the animal-like shining of Geraldine's eyes in the dark" (32), and J. B. Beer in *Coleridge the Visionary* (London, 1959), cites an alteration in Coleridge's hand in a volume of his poems:

> . . . and full in view,
> Behold! her bosom and half her side—
> It was dark & rough as the Sea-Wolf's hide
> A sight to dream of, not to tell!

Beer gives his source as Coleridge, *Poems*, 1828, II, 54. (MS amendment by Coleridge to copy now in Fitzwilliam Museum, Cambridge.) See Beer, 191 and n. Basler's observation of animal nature in Geraldine and Beer's speculations about Geraldine as werewolf (190-91) are both perceptive and support the relationship of Geraldine to the mastiff bitch.

[30] PWC, I, 221, lines 145-53.

[31] For a thoroughly conventional precedent, consider Sin's address to Satan in Milton's *Paradise Lost*:

> Hast thou forgot me then, and do I seem
> Now in thine eye so foul, once deemed so fair
> In Heav'n, when at th'Assembly, and in sight
> Of all the Seraphim with thee combin'd
> In bold conspiracy against Heav'ns King,
> All on a sudden miserable pain
> Surpris'd thee, dim thine eyes, and dizzie swumm
> In darkness, while thy head flames thick and fast
> Threw forth, till on the left side op'ning wide,
> Likest to thee in shape and count'nance bright,
> Then shining heav'nly fair, a Goddess arm'd
> Out of thy head I sprung; amazement seis'd
> All th' Host of Heav'n; back they recoild affraid
> At first, and call'd me *Sin*, and for a Sign
> Portentous held me; but familiar grown,
> I pleas'd, and with attractive graces won
> The most averse, thee chiefly, who full oft
> Thy self in me thy perfect image viewing
> Becam'st enamour'd, and such joy thou took'st
> With me in secret, that my womb conceiv'd
> A growing burden. . . .
>
> . . . .
>   Pensive here I sat
> Alone, but long I sat not, till my womb
> Pregnant by thee, and now excessive grown
> Prodigious motion felt and rueful throes.
> At last this odious offspring whom thou seest
> Thine own begotten, breaking violent way
> Tore through my entrails, that with fear and pain
> Distorted, all my nether shape thus grew

Transform'd: but he my inbred enemie
Forth issu'd, brandishing his fatal Dart
  Made to destroy: I fled, and cry'd out *Death* (*The Poetical Works
of John Milton*, ed. H.C. Beeching [London, 1935], 219-20, lines 747-
86).

Milton's adaptation and expansion of the Zeus-Athene myth is a bril-
liant example of literary elaboration of fantasies that are similar to Coleridge's fantasies; and the elaboration is of course at least as complex.
The pattern of autoeroticism, accompanied by fantasies of usurpation,
of double sexuality, and of punishment in the form of headache, blindness, and death, ought to be investigated in Milton's work. The birth and
seduction of Sin are exactly parallel to the nympholeptic quest in Romantic poetry, and specifically to Coleridge's search for the heart within
his heart. The phrase "thick and fast" in line 754 in the passage quoted
turns up in "The Nightingale" (PWC, I, 265, line 45) as modifier of
the nightingale's "warble," and this in a poem that quotes from "Il Pen-
seroso" the line with which Milton describes the nightingale's song as
"Most musicall, most melancholy!" (Milton, 24, line 62). Coleridge's
footnote (in *Lyrical Ballads*) to the quotation is: "This passage in Milton
possesses an excellence far superior to that of mere description; it is spoken in the character of the melancholy Man, and has therefore a *dramatic*
propriety. The Author makes this remark, to rescue himself from the
charge of having alluded with levity to a line in Milton; a charge than
which none could be more painful to him, except perhaps that of having
ridiculed his Bible" (PWC, I, 264 n.). The image of death "brandishing
his fatal Dart" recalls the letter to Poole recounting his father's death.

[32] The relevant details in Gillman's account of Coleridge's plan for the
conclusion of the poem surround the quest of Bracy the bard for Sir Roland de Vaux. Bracy arrives at the place where Sir Roland's castle is alleged to be and finds that the place has been flooded and the castle—and
presumably Sir Roland—utterly washed away. *Cf.* the *Chanson de Roland* which also presents a fruitless quest.

[33] See Woodring's discussion of *Osorio* as an attack against political
tyranny: "On balance, the author does not seem to include himself among
the guilty" (205). Bracy is a perfect expression of Coleridge's view of
himself as a man in whom action and poetic insight are incompatible.
Cf. his comments on the character of Hamlet. See also *infra*, Chapters
V, VI, and VII, for discussions of this incompatibility in *Kubla Khan*,
the *Rime*, the "abstruse research," and the *Dejection* ode.

[34] PWC, I, 218-19, lines 81-97.

[35] Robert F. Fleissner, in "The Mystical Meaning of Five: A Notelet on 'Kubla Khan,'" *English Studies*, XLVI (1965), nos. 1-6, 45, commenting on the emendation from the Crewe manuscript reading "twice six miles" to "twice five miles" in the received version of *Kubla Khan*, suggests that Coleridge had "an intuitive perception of the mystical qualities inherent in the Golden Number. Called Aphrodite's number by the pagans because it was the fusion of the first male and first female digits, five attained exceptional recognition in Pythagorean mythology . . . Its presence in Nature, most obviously shall we say in the five fingers of the human hand, has its counterpart in religious ritual (the five wounds of Christ, for example)." Fleissner uses this fascinating information to support his reading of "five" in *Kubla Khan* as "a finite number linked up to the idea of infinity;" but he makes no connection between "Aphrodite's number" as a male-female fusion and the submerged sexuality or quasi-sexuality of the poem (for which see *infra*, Chapter V). The connection seems particularly relevant to *Christabel* as well, and although Fleissner does not make it clear how Coleridge could have been "intuitively aware" of the number's mystical qualities unless he had read some of Fleissner's sources (CN, 1961, and CL, II, 1083, provide evidence that he had read one of those sources—Browne's *Garden of Cyrus*—as pointed out by Kathleen Raine in an article in the *Sewanee Review*, LXXII, 626-642 [cited in Fleissner] by 1804, but there is nothing to show that he had read it earlier than that), it is possible that the word "mystical" is not so helpful a term as "mythical" might be in the circumstances. Like other ancient and durable equivalences, this one is powerfully suggestive of an unconscious fantasy: the sexual confusion that accompanies autoeroticism. Fleissner chooses the image of five fingers as being "most obviously" an example of the number "in Nature." It seems most unlikely— given the present state of literary criticism in which two such journals rarely cross the same desk—that he had read in the *International Journal of Psychoanalysis*, XLV (April-July, 1964), 411-425, Eli Marcovitz's "Bemoaning the Lost Dream: Coleridge's 'Kubla Khan' and Addiction," a paper presented in 1961 to the Philadelphia Association for Psychoanalysis. Marcovitz, after examining the Crewe manuscript, concludes that the emendation "five" must have proceeded from an unconscious association with the five fingers. He suggests an image cluster revealing a nursing fantasy: "hands, mouth, and mother's breast." Marcovitz's article is far from careful (he believes that Francis Coleridge died in 1799),

but it is interesting in connection with Fleissner's association and the properties of "Aphrodite's number."

[36] PWC, I, 220, lines 121-22.

[37] *Ibid.*, I, 390, line 23. *Cf. ibid.*, 225, lines 292-97, 226, lines 311-31.

[38] *Ibid.*, I, 216, lines 29-30.

[39] See Bostetter, 125, 131. But he finds evidence of sadism only in Geraldine and Sir Leoline. Mario Praz in *The Romantic Agony* (Oxford, 1951) presents a fairly clear analysis of literary expression of the Romantic pleasure that is to be found in the contemplation of suffering women, but with only a cryptic and oblique reference to *Christabel* as "a fairy transposition of a Lesbian love-affair." (477)

[40] Bostetter (130) finds that ". . . *Christabel* is no mere Gothic tale but the dramatic exploration of the nature of evil and its ambiguous interrelation with good."

[41] PWC, I, 216, lines 23-30.

[42] *Ibid.*, I, 225, lines 292-97.

[43] *Ibid.*, I, 220, lines 123-34.

[44] See Praz and Bostetter.

[45] PWC, I, 226, lines 311-18.

[46] Angus is only partly right in reading loss here as loss simply of mother love.

[47] PWC, I, 216, line 19.

[48] The tree in myth and folklore is conventionally a symbol of male divinity. The mistletoe is rarely found on an English oak tree, so that its presence here connotes some deviation in Christabel's sexual nature. In addition, the mistletoe was, according to Pliny, the source of cure for sexual sterility among the Druids and figured prominently in their fertility rituals. As ornamentation, the mistletoe in folklore represents the male genitalia. For a discussion of sexual ambiguity in *Christabel* see Ware, 339-40, 343-5.

[49] PWC, I, 230, lines 447-50.

[50] *Ibid.*, I, 230, lines 451-56.

[51] *Ibid.*, I, 230, lines 457-62.

[52] *Ibid.*, I, 224, lines 250-54.

[53] *Ibid.*, I, 224.

[54] *Ibid.*, I, 224, lines 255-62.

[55] *Ibid.*, I, 224.

[56] *Loc. cit.*

[57] *Loc. cit.*

[58] PWC, I, 215.

[59] See especially Elisabeth Schneider, *Coleridge, Opium, and Kubla Khan* (Chicago, 1953), 106-09, for a perceptive discussion of Coleridge's wide swings between self-doubt and self-assertion. See also Max F. Schulz, "Coleridge's 'Apologetic' Prefaces," *Tulane Studies in English*, XI (1961), 53-64.

[60] Ware, 345-6.

[61] Bostetter, 132: "The 'Conclusion' [of *Christabel*] is a symbolic gesture of frustration, a confession of defeat. . . . The creation of poetry . . . forced him to look deep into himself, in a self-contemplation that became finally too painful to bear because it contradicted all that he wanted to believe about himself and his universe."

Chapter Five

[1] In a massive effort to explain the poem, John Livingston Lowes produced *The Road to Xanadu* (Boston, 1927), which traces Coleridge's reading habits and demonstrates that writers associate literary details to each other and to the details of their own work, but without providing any help in the attempt to understand why Coleridge was attracted to certain literary sources rather than to others. N. P. Stallknecht's article, "The Moral of *The Ancient Mariner*" (PMLA, 1932), reprinted in *Strange Seas of Thought* (Durham, N.C., 1945), 141-71, began a vogue for Christian interpretation of the poem that reached a climax in Robert Penn Warren's essay and annotation in his edition of the *Rime* (New York, 1946) which combine elements of Christian allegory, neoplatonism, and psychoanalysis. Maud Bodkin in *Archetypal Patterns in Poetry* (Oxford, 1934) had already made her impressionistic study in a Jungian onslaught in which she relies on such evidence as her own dreams. Freudian readings of the poem are of two types, both of which still need to be brought into balance with each other. One type emphasizes literary interpretation and includes such works as G. Wilson Knight's *The Starlit Dome* (New York, 1941) and Kenneth Burke's *Philosophy of Literary Form* (Baton Rouge, 1941). The other type appears in psychoanalytic journals and emphasizes Freudian interpreta-

tion. Two recent writers who have attempted to synthesize literary and Freudian techniques are Bostetter (108-17) and Angus.

[2] Anna Letitia Barbauld (1743-1825), the wife of the Rev. R. Barbauld, was a popular writer who objected to Coleridge that the *Rime* lacked a moral. In reply, Coleridge observed that the poem's chief fault was "the obtrusion of the moral sentiment so openly on the reader as a principle or cause of action in a work of such pure imagination." (TT, May 31, 1830, 87)

[3] David Beres, in "A Dream, a Vision, and a Poem: a Psychoanalytic Study of the Origins of the Rime of the Ancient Mariner," *International Journal of Psychoanalysis*, XXXII (1951), 97-116, makes such an error in quite simply equating the mariner's destruction of the albatross with Coleridge's unconscious aggressive fantasies about his mother. Coleridge was at pains to distinguish between allegory, which he found a deliberate one-to-one equivalence, and symbol, which "is characterized by a translucence of the special in the individual, or of the general in the special, or of the universal in the general. . . . It always partakes of the reality which it renders intelligible; and while it enunciates the whole, abides itself as a living part in that unity, of which it is the representative." From *The Statesman's Manual*, cited in Kathleen Coburn, *The Inquiring Spirit* (London, 1951), 103-04. He held further that allegory "cannot be otherwise than spoken consciously; whereas in [symbol] it is very possible that the general truth may be working unconsciously in the writer's mind." From *Miscellaneous Criticism*, ed. Thomas Middleton Raysor (London, 1936), 33.

[4] The phrase occurs in PWC, I, 101, line 26, and is picked up by Warren, in his interpretation of the *Rime*, as the object of sacramental vision that is violated by the mariner.

[5] This is of course not the eternal life of the Christian soul but rather something like the picture of the Struldbrugs that Swift drew in *Gulliver's Travels*. Cf. *The Wanderings of Cain*, PWC, I, 285-92.

[6] PWC, I, 193-94, lines 187-94.

[7] The Teiresias myth is variously reported. It is significant that in one version, which has been attractive to T. S. Eliot, he is not only blinded as a result of forbidden visual knowledge but is also experienced in both male and female sexuality.

[8] Daniel A. Huebsch, "Psychoanalysis and Eye Disturbances," *Psychoanalytic Review*, XVIII (1931), 166-80.

[9] DWJ, I, 74.

[10] CN, I, 848 4.123.

[11] Coburn notices a "falling off in Coleridge's trips to Grasmere and the frequency of the Wordsworths' visits to the Lloyds" before this date (CN, I, 834 4.117 n.).

[12] See for example Hanson and Chambers.

[13] CN, I, 848 4.123 n.: "On Coleridge and his dreams a volume might be written. Swollen eye-lids and other bodily pains frequently go with them, and the figure of the menacing pursuer (or pursuers), usually feminine, is almost constant."

[14] *Cf.* the actual pallor of Sara Hutchinson as it is reported by Coleridge's daughter. *Supra*, Chapter IV.

[15] The work done by Elisabeth Schneider would seem to have dispelled forever the legend Coleridge created about the composition of *Kubla Khan* during an opium dream. But as late as 1959 J. B. Beer is inclined to believe it: "But can we accept the statement that the poem was composed in a 'Reverie'? The point is a difficult one, but the various name-fabrications, and a certain inconsequence, superficially, in the poem's action, suggest that the poem was in fact composed in something less than a state of full consciousness. . . . we may well wonder whether the laudanum might not have been taken for help in writing poetry: but this is an issue which is unlikely ever to be clarified." (201) He goes on to offer evidence to support "The idea that very intricate mental processes can take place in states of imperfect consciousness . . ." (202)

[16] Schulz, 114; E. H. W. Meyerstein, "Completeness of *Kubla Kahn*," *Times Literary Supplement,* October 30, 1937, 803; Humphry House, *Coleridge* (London, 1953), 114-22, *inter alia.*

[17] See especially House and Beer.

[18] Donald T. Bliss and Hilde S. Bliss, in "Coleridge's *Kubla Khan*," *American Imago,* VI (1949), 261-73, present some interesting psycho-analytic insights (including the reading of the dome as a symbol of femaleness), but in a general context of one-to-one equivalences. See also Marcovitz, Angus, and Gerald E. Enscoe, "Ambivalence in 'Kubla Khan': The Cavern and the Dome," *Bucknell Review,* XII, i, 29-36.

[19] PWC, I, 297, lines 1-11.

[20] He "creates" her himself, just as Zeus creates Athene and as the Romantic poets "create" the "ideal" object of the nympholeptic quest, in narcissistic projection of the self.

[21] Schulz, 122.

[22] *Cf.* the "ruined tower" in "Love," PWC, I, 331, line 8.

[23] PWC, I, 297-98, lines 12-36.

[24] See Praz, *passim.*

[25] PWC, I, 390, line 23.

[26] *Ibid.*, 298, lines 37-54.

[27] Angus sees the failure to revive the maid within him, again, simply as lost mother love.

[28] See Bliss and Bliss, 263.

[29] *E.g.*, Beer, *passim.*

[30] Schulz, "Coleridge's 'Apologetic' Prefaces."

[31] Schulz, in *The Poetic Voices*, also considers it a dream poem, but in a different sense. See 114-24. See also Schneider, *op. cit.*

[32] *Biographia Literaria*, ed. J. Shawcross (London, 1954), I, 202.

Chapter Six

[1] The most recent full-length studies are James V. Baker, *The Sacred River: Coleridge's Theory of the Imagination* (Louisiana, 1957) and J. A. Appleyard, *Coleridge's Philosophy of Literature: The Development of a Concept of Poetry*, 1791-1819 (Cambridge, Mass., 1965). See also Meyer H. Abrams, *The Mirror and the Lamp* (New York, 1953), *passim*, and René Wellek, *A History of Modern Criticism* (New Haven, 1955), II, 157-81.

[2] See Wellek for full discussion and excellent bibliography on this point. But see also Appleyard, *op. cit.*, for another point of view.

[3] Ernst Cassirer, *The Philosophy of the Enlightenment*, trans. Fritz C. A. Koelln and James P. Pettegrove (Boston, 1955).

[4] See *Biographia Literaria*, I, Chapters V, VI, VII, VIII, and IX.

[5] Cassirer, *op. cit.*, 124.

[6] *Ibid.*, 164.

[7] See Walter Greiner, "Deutsche Einflüsse auf die Dichtungstheorie von Samuel Taylor Coleridge," *Die Neueren Sprachen*, Neue Folge, II (1960), 57-65, for a discussion of the influence of Johann Nicolas Tetens on Coleridge's esthetic theories.

[8] *Biographia Literaria*, I, 107.

[9] Cassirer, 316. The Shaftesbury quotation is from *Characteristics*, ed. J. M. Robertson (London, 1900), I, 136.

[10] CL, II, 1034.

[11] Baker is puzzled by the fact that "in spite of his awareness of association and the unconscious as potential allies of the poet, he seriously underestimated the power of memory and the 'deep well' to effect a sea change. For a man who profited by it so much, he was strangely ungracious concerning the alchemy of the unconscious." (227) He was indeed ungracious, and no wonder.

[12] *Biographia Literaria*, I, 202.

[13] See *infra*, 105.

[14] *Biographia*, II, 212 n.

[15] See *supra, passim*, for discussions of the other two means: filial relationships with other men is one and the other is poetry-making.

[16] *Biographia*, I, 10.

[17] PWC, I, 367, lines 87-93.

[18] *Biographia*, I, 185-86.

[19] See discussion of *Christabel, Kubla Khan*, and the *Rime, supra.*

[20] *Biographia*, I, 183.

[21] More than twenty years elapsed between the composition of *The Aeolian Harp* and the publication of the *Biographia*. As a matter of fact, his defensive attitudes toward religion never left him.

[22] PWC, I, 102, lines 49-64.

[23] Lionel Trilling, *Matthew Arnold* (New York, 1939), 83-4.

[24] CL, II, 831.

[25] See especially *Christabel*.

[26] *E.g.*, Kenneth Burke and James V. Baker.

[27] The first followed his father's death and the second followed Frank's death.

[28] HL, 155.

[29] *Wordsworthian and Other Studies*, 65-66.

[30] *Op. cit.*, 61.

[31] See ChL, 194 ff.

[32] It was at this time that Wordsworth busied himself with straightening out his affairs with Annette Vallon in order to clear the slate for his marriage to Mary Hutchinson.

[33] Dorothy, as usual, interested herself in her brother's problems at least as much as he did. See DWJ, I, 103-83.

[34] George Whalley, *Coleridge and Sara Hutchinson* (Toronto, 1955). Hereinafter referred to as WhC. Whalley's dating of Wordsworth's first recorded letter to Annette should apparently be corrected to January 26. *Cf.* WhC, 42 and DWJ, I, 102.

[35] WhC, 42-3.

[36] F. W. Bateson, in *Wordsworth: A Re-interpretation* (London, 1956), 143-63, speculates that Dorothy may have been an unconscious obstacle to Wordsworth's relationship with Annette, and suggests that the marriage to Mary was Wordsworth's attempt to escape from the mutual incestuous love between Wordsworth and his sister that was beginning to threaten his consciousness. No one who reads the passages from Dorothy's journal cited in Bateson's book can reasonably argue that he is wrong about this. See DWJ, I, 103-83.

[37] See the exchange of letters between Coleridge and the Wordsworths as referred to in DWJ, I, 103-121. The period between Wordsworth's January 26 letter to Annette and the first week of March was filled with correspondence; Coleridge's letters were unhappy. On March 19 Coleridge finally arrived for a visit at Grasmere: "Coleridge came in—his eyes were a little swollen with the wind. I was much affected with the sight of him, he seemed half stupefied." (DWJ, I, 127) On March 21, Coleridge left Grasmere and wrote no letters to the Wordsworths for the week that preceded their visit to Keswick on March 28—the visit that ended April 4, the day of the evening on which Coleridge composed the *Letter to [Sara]*.

Chapter Seven

[1] WhC, 155. All quotations from *A Letter to——* are taken from this source. See also DES and CL, II, 790-98.

[2] *Lap* is an alteration of *arme* in the image found in the ballad.

[3] All quotations from the ballad are taken from Thomas Percy, *Reliques of Ancient English Poetry*, ed. Henry B. Wheatley (London, 1891), I, 100 ff.

[4] Is there a latent pun here indicating kingship, which is always vulnerable to usurpation?

5 *Cf.* Coleridge's complaint of Wordsworth's cruelty in the context of the dream in which his eye is pulled out by a woman.

6 Schulz, 140, is the only writer who has suggested that the extensive revision of the poem into its received form was anything but literary craftsmanship exercised to make it less personal and therefore more artful (in a good sense). The result is of course better literary art, but the motivation was clearly the fear of the revelation of unconscious material in the first draft. See also Yarlott, *op. cit.*

7 *Cf. Kubla Khan.*

8 This is an interesting reference to *Tintern Abbey*, indicating some confusion between Sara and Dorothy.

9 See CN, I, 1242 255 n.: " 'First Stone layed by Sara on Thursday March 26, 1801. So it remained till Saturday noon, Octr. 10 1801—when between the hours of 12 and 2, William Wordsworth and his Sister—with S. T. Coleridge built it, to wit, all the stonework; with the foot-stones— we being all there in hope and prayer, that Mary with Tom Hutchinson had then already set off, or were setting off, from Gallow Hill—on their road to Grasmere—God in Heaven bless her and him too. October 10th 10 days before my Birthday, when I shall be 29 years old—Eheu *vixi!!* S. T. Coleridge.

'Saturday Noon from ¼ past 12 to 2 (Octob. 10. 1801) Numbers 1, 2, and 4, were built up compleatly* the Seat of which little Sara had layed the first stone so long back on Thursday, March 26th 1801. dear Mary, I wish you may be on the road to us. *All but the moss cushion. S.T.C.' MS note on the flyleaves of Friedrich Matthisson's *Gedichte* (Zürich 1797) in VCL."

10 WhC reads *the*, but the facsimile facing 156 plainly shows *thy*.

11 Her "guileless Letter" has not survived, nor has his own.

12 There is no evidence for anything more fervent than a kiss between Coleridge and Sara.

13 See discussion of *Christabel, supra*, Chapter IV. See also Praz.

14 PWC, I, 368, line 115.

15 *Lonesome* reads *heathy* in the *Letter*. The change intensifies the appeal to pity.

16 *Bitter* reads *utter* in the *Letter*. This is another change which intensifies self-pity.

17 PWC, I, 368, line 125.

[18] *Kubla Khan* is the most direct expression of the equivalence between literary elaboration and sexual release.

[19] This line, the recollection of paradise lost, is an afterthought, inserted above the next line.

[20] Incorporation is an emotional process by means of which the child takes on personality characteristics of the parent.

[21] The equivalence is not unusual. There are any number of figures of speech in English that express confusion between artistic creation and procreation or between thought and sexuality. "Brain child" is one.

[22] See TT, Sept. 1, 1832: "The truth is, a great mind must be androgynous."

[23] *Life* is inserted above the line.

[24] See Suther, 13-24, for an informed discussion of writers who blame either the "abstruse research" or some generalized character weakness for Coleridge's feeling failure. Suther disagrees with both camps and replaces their theories with his own theological view of the difficulty.

[25] Griggs's brackets.

[26] CL, II, 902.

[27] CL, I, 479.

[28] *Ibid.*, I, 449 n.

[29] *Ibid.*, I, 449.

[30] *Ibid.*, I, 490.

[31] Griggs's brackets, here and throughout passage.

[32] Coleridge's parentheses. For some psychoanalytic comments on the *liebestod* fantasy, see Cecil D. Murray, "A Recent Case of Dying Together," *Psychoanalytic Review*, XVIII (1931), 63-68.

[33] PWC, I, 314.

[34] See *supra*, Chapter II.

[35] *And a* reads in the received version *A fair*. See PWC, I, 365, line 54.

[36] See *supra*, 119, 124-25.

[37] PWC, I, 365, line 66.

[38] This line and the one that precedes it are inserted above the next line.

[39] The phrase is inserted.

Index

THE KENT STUDIES IN ENGLISH

F